Eagerly We Burn

ALSO BY BARRY HILL

The Schools (1977)
A Rim of Blue: Stories (1978)
Near the Refinery: a novella (1980)
Headlocks and Other Stories (1983)
The Best Picture: a novel (1988)
Raft: Poems 1983–1990 (1990)
Sitting In (1991)
Ghosting William Buckley: a poem (1993)
The Rock: Travelling to Uluru (1997)
The Inland Sea: Poems (2001)
Broken Song: T G H Strehlow and Aboriginal Possession (2002)
The Enduring Rip: A History of Queenscliffe (2004)
The War Sonnets (2007)
Necessity: Poems 1996–2006 (2007)
Four Lines East (2007)
As We Draw Ourselves (2008)
Lines for Birds (2011)
Naked Clay: Drawing from Lucian Freud (2012)
Peacemongers (2014)
Grass Hut Work (2016)
Reason & Lovelessness: Essays, encounters, reviews 1980-2017 (2018)

Barry Hill

Eagerly We Burn

*Selected Poems
1980–2018*

Shearsman Books

First published in the United Kingdom in 2019 by
Shearsman Books
50 Westons Hill Drive
Emersons Green
BRISTOL
BS16 7DF

Shearsman Books Ltd Registered Office
30–31 St. James Place, Mangotsfield, Bristol BS16 9JB
(this address not for correspondence)

www.shearsman.com

ISBN 978-1-84861-608-0

Copyright © Barry Hill, 2019.

The right of Barry Hill to be identified as the author
of this work has been asserted by him in accordance with the
Copyrights, Designs and Patents Act of 1988.
All rights reserved.

CONTENTS

Recent Poems

That Beautiful Black Horse	11
Kind Fire	12
Her Favourite Munch	13
Beloved Historian at Home	14
Plum Juice	15
Badly Mothered, Burning Chaos	16
Politics	19
No Eye, No Ear, No Tongue	21
Glove	23
New Alice Springs Poems	24
Ready	27

Grass Hut Work (2016)

Turnips in Kyoto	28
On Getting to Grips with the Heart Sutra	32
All Over the Body	36
Unholy	38
Bashō's Sin	39
Rough Notes	41
Almost Forgetting	42
Untitled	43
Poor Reason	43
Boy O Boy	44
Like Grass	45
Crazi Iris	46
To Speak of Tragedy	47
Lines Found in my Father's Hiroshima Folder	48
The Loveliest Things	50

Naked Clay: Drawing from Lucian Freud (2012)

Boy with Pigeon	51
Girl in Bed	52

Narcissus	53
Girl with White Dog	54
Fathers and Daughters	56
Woman Smiling	57
Colour of a Breast	58
Naked Child Laughing	59
Man's Head	60
Mother: portraits	61
Beneath	64
Studio Songs	67
The Roar; Reflection	69
Lying by the Rags	70
Eggs	71
Esther	72
Painter Working, Reflection	73
Naked Man: Back View	75
Benefits Supervisor by Lion Carpet	76
Daphne	77
Painter Surprised by a Naked Admirer	78
from Magnanimity	79

Lines for Birds (2011)

Thrush Summer	80
Eagerly We Burn	81
Masked Woodswallows	83
War Music	84
Our Winter Desert	85
What We Didn't See	87
Truth	88
Warm Far North	89
Gannets	91
On the Brilliant Engagement of Paradise Rifle Birds	93
The Feast	94
Vow 3 a.m.	95
Space Travel	96
The Wave	98
Redstart	100

Burning Eggs	102
Passion	103
Messiaen's Music for the Reed-Warbler	105
Kite / *Tobi*	111

Four Lines East (2009)

Raven City	112
Under the Sign of Necessity	113
from At Varanasi	115
Himalayan Fire	116
Reading the Diamond Sutra at Chiang Mai	118

As We Draw Ourselves (2008)

Green River	120
Crossing St Peter's Square…	121
Disegno for Michelangelo	123
At Assisi	127
Homecoming	130
Reading on the Darkening Plain	131
Sex in Japan	132
Dojo	134

Necessity: Poems 1996-2006 (2007)

Old Photo: The Union Buries	135
A Mackerel Green Sea	136
I know a Poet with a Gun	138
from War Sonnets	140
from Flint: Gramsci in Prison	143
Overture: Getting The Revolution Straight	148
Poland	151

The Inland Sea (2001)

Honey Ant	158
Noon	158

Ribs	159
Songs and Escarpments	160
Underground Rivers Running	162
Riverbed Song	163
Back	164
Road Train	165

Ghosting William Buckley (1993)

Good Ship Calcutta	166
Escaping	168
At a Pinch	172
Magpie	174
Eel	174
Promiscuous	175
Tattoo	178
Koim	178
On Civilization's Platter	179

Raft (1990)

Dune	181
Downpour	182
Banquet	183
Hope	184
from My Daughter's Blood	185
Idea of Absence	187
Horticulture	188
Dim Sim Time	189
Rope	190
Notes & Acknowledgements	192

for Rose, her Song

That Beautiful Black Horse

It's too early to be fearful, or angry.
When the sun comes up it's going to feel colder.
The scum at the edge of Swan Bay will look white
but grubby, the fast water still inky.

The wind will feel like it's come across the frosty Nullarbor
but it hasn't
it's just whipped up
and fallen upon us from the Antarctic.

Lend me your beanie.

I'm carrying a candle
one of many on a kitchen tray
in the dark, step by step, a glow under my chin.

The ten thousand jam jars
(we scrounged as many as we could)
the ten thousand candle flames

and the lights are placed on the black road
for a leap of the imagination:
composing the word PEACE

at the boom gate
on the road to the secret base before dawn.

Now what?

By the paddy wagon, the horse stamps and snorts.

Kind Fire

i.m. Seamus Heaney

Not the digging of potatoes
but the forging of iron implements
produced those shoulders
and the biceps I pressed—
a boy's hand on the father's bulge
a swelling roughly the same shape

as the hammer's head
I still have, along with his chisel
as thick as my wrist was thin.
Tools hand-made, part-time
in time stolen from the boss
at the Victorian Railways Erecting Shop—

one of the great sheds among many
in the long dry grass with the Scotch
thistles out past the Abattoirs
on the way to the back beach:
ribbed sand, soldier crabs, an oily creek, eels
a bike ride from home

me sitting on the little padded seat
the iron-framed perch between his arms
near the handle bars
his breath a bellows on my neck
his kind fire always there
as he peddled me into the Southerly.

Her Favourite Munch

i.m. Beverley Farmer

She tells you again, as you arrive once more, that she is dead
already: she died yesterday or the day before. Or both.

You used to say: I think I know the feeling
(after a birthday, sleeping pills, a big dumb night…)

Glib. Wash your mouth out.
Now you say: I just wish I could bury you.

There. Knee to knee, let that sink in.
Bury you was the kindest thing you could think to say.

You did not have to think. You just said it.
Thoughtfully she heard it, as would a crow in her fig tree.

There are scraps of food on her lovely upper lip.
The other day you clipped her fingernails.

Gothic, and as greasy as the seat of her walking frame…
You wondered about her toes, zipped up in pink.

Like dyed dead rabbits. But you are not
her keeper, you never married her, let the nurses smirk.

Anyway, she intends (an odd word) a cremation.
In the absence of a sky burial, you could set her alight.

Remember the friend who said she was a pure flame?
The walker's so filthy it would go up in a tic…

Dusk. And she's still in her pyjamas. This morning
she declared a holiday. No one need touch her today.

Huge, cobalt blue, Matisse flowers on silently
screaming snow white. She might even be enjoying

the look of that look. You could turn up in a dressing gown
—stand the other side of the bed, just like her favourite Munch.

Beloved Historian at Home

For Hugh and Patsy Stretton

He cannot remember a line of his great works
or my name, but most days he locates his toothbrush.

And he can, still, turn to his wife
who finds him there in his well of love.

Plum Juice

Without realising
        I turned the page
                with wet fingers
on my new copy
        of Du Fu
                smearing *The Sick Horse*.
Later, when I thought them dry
                I came to *Facing the Snow*
the pictures he painted
        crackling
                with pure lament:
Above the battlefield
many new ghosts are crying;
        steeped in sorrow
a lone old man is chanting.

        The ladle lies useless
the wine jar toppled over;
        the stove grows cold,
red embers slowly fading…

And still my touch was dark
        a purply red
                an indelible ink
my brush swollen
        to write an end
                to our running wars.
    No news comes
from anywhere this winter.
    In empty air
a sad old man is writing.

Badly Mothered, Blazing Chaos

i.m. Sam Hamill

Your rugged smile, Sam.
It had been around O
it had been around.
You had Utah grit between your teeth.

Worn down at fifteen
you cleared off to Haight-Ashbury
where you got yourself two 'little habits'—
a fist-full of poetry here, a load of smack there…

Then, half a century later, you land here!
To sup at a safe antipodean table
like some new artificial paradise—
with us 'being kind' (as you said of me and my wife)

to our post-op guest:
a man weakened but still chewing
the fat of poetry and politics and socialism.
You were the first Yank I'd heard say 'socialism'.

Seemed we'd both arrived at a good place.

I asked you, apropos the youthful street life
the muggings, the jail terms
if you were 'still an arsehole'.
Your grin could have filled a flagon.

Today, you would have been 75
just weeks before me, another month
breaking onto another beach of poetry:
black wave after black wave of blank verse
Zen ruminations and whatnot—
little tsunamis of hope, literary effects

and paraphrase, Classical homage, subservience
to truculent beauty in our own idiom.

All the while casting a cold eye on the college kids—
their fathers, the bankers and industrialists
the arms-manufacturers, the gun-keepers
and the gatekeepers. The anti-socialist cunts…

But we loved women, we really did.
Good women were what we needed
good cunt or no good cunt (we're drunk again!).
Fellow cunt-worshipers, not mother-fuckers.

Anything but harm a mother, and that's the truth.

The mothers who harmed us came on this earth
to teach us some truth, that's the truth too.
They taught us to treat all things as equal.
They led us into all manner of translation.

Remember when I asked you why
Bashō left that kid by the side of the road?
The cruelty of haiku! More had to be said!
I was uncomprehending, incredulous: you far less so.

We get what we get the way a good line
finds its full-stop. Only to start over again
as pipings on pipings became our life—
Taoists while hardly knowing and

trying to resist the disconsolate
making this line better than that
(or at least as good as that jerk's). Anyway
a strong line does not permit a man to put himself down…

When we left the table I held up some Chinese.
'Aw', you drawled, 'I'm not working on that right now.'

Wish I'd had a line from your Chuang Tzu:
The blazing chaos is the light that guides the sage.

And to think: back then, the authorities thought
they were giving you a clear choice:
'Do real time, Hamill, or join the Marines'.

And that cleaner of latrines in Okinawa
the old man who showed you the interiors
of temples… When did it hit you that
secret teachings include powers to set up type?

Behind me the candle burns, Sam.

Politics

You might need to take up karate again
If only to take off your own head
In the mirror of fake news

The lies are so thick on the ground
You can hear the crunching underfoot
Slugs galore, slugs born in sophist throats

Worse than sophists. You'll need to
Wring or break—one strike—their necks:
Speech has little to do with it

It's as if they drink *Round Up*
They munch each other's fingernails
Which the best have pulled out

They have stopped screaming
And you can't scream these days
But you went through a recent phase

Or phrase, the framing of your abuse
Animus, homicidal desires, new insights:
'To love thy neighbour is an act of aggression'

You know the goody two shoes teaching
On anger, revenge, blood lust, what you want
Is to get your hands on their tiny minds

And cruel eyes, fingers into those eyes—
An emergency strike, forget the etiquette, yes
Blind them and bind them, take them out…

Ever think you would be like this?
Thank them then. They have shown you something
They have drawn you out of the Pathos Self

Osu, Sempai. Fight freely around the empty bowl
Bow and strike, strike and bow. Go to it again
Be the vital young clown you thought you were

Work your way around the floor
As the nightmare roars, revive right ceremony
Perform the Fire Ode, abandon funeral rites

No eye, No ear, No tongue

What's happened to those *murmured conversations*?
The gentle links between verses, words, whispers?

All that might happen under a lowly thatched roof
after the ten thousand thoughts pass through

in a single night, and which the morning
brings the light into, gently gently lifting shadows

as heart-mind departs from moth-wings
assembles in units of a poem to be woven

together by men attuned to each other, their buds
and stems of poems, and to the spirit of enlightenment.

How could you have travelled so far into darkness?
Some poems, gleefully thrummed, expel illumination.

They are acts of war. They dwell in vanity
can shame you to death, banish you to Bardo—

One false note and you have no poem of worth
or to speak of, you have kinky murders at midnight.

I think (is this the link?) (I dimly realise now)
A poem mangled in wilful conception

gives the risky game away: it reveals a desire
to be priest above all else, some vain character in black

a spirit failing in himself, in health, faith in service:
someone cruel to dogs, a beast of a man who kicks

living things out of his way, who thinks
nothing of treading on a harmless cockroach…

In the time of poet-monk Shinkei
the character for dog was written

on the new-born's brow as a charm
to protect the child from evil.

Your poem had no feeling for dog or cockroach
so in love with itself is your word-spirit.

You remain fond of the poem even as you feel its evil.
Who knows what *minima moralia* will fire you next?

All you knew while writing
was that one dark link would lead to the next…

Now try to find your way back…
Wordlessly if need be, no eye, no ear, no tongue…

The Glove

For Ronald Farron-Price

A friend
one who Pound would have called
       an old man with beautiful manners
              a Beethoven man
dwelling in the divine structures
       from the beginning
              to the end of his time
was telling me of his present, slow days
       of how his mornings
              some of his loveliest time is spent
              fingering…

I was at a loss.
       Poets have no word for what
              he was intimating….
Except perhaps to say—
       like choreography for hands
       like a dance of heart-mind or

       approaching a form of emptiness
       like touching fullness on the shoulder
             having it turn around…

Cross these out. Stay dumb. Just
       leave him be next time you meet.
Quietly imagine yourself
       slipping your own hand
              into a god's glove.

New Alice Springs Poems

Right Love

Who has written
with right love
about this hard light?

It flicks pebbles, sharpens
reeds, makes ghost gums
amorous for dance.

In Hidden Valley—
atomic clarity of dusk.
They stand around
not looking
as we drive up.
Kids with little salt lakes
glinting on their upper lips.

We are there to help.
We will take your rubbish.
Just bring
as the sun sinks
the bag of rattling cans
that *sound* like the light.

In Hidden Valley
I got caught in the glare
the amplifying net it cast
each of us with pores open
glances shooting past
the whole camp under daytime stars.

Then, back on the bitumen
the night time slump
the light no longer peeling
off you, or them
the conversation about them
starting all over again.

No Maggots Today

She had gales in her
bosom and belly
a sashay rolled
into a clap of mirth

an almost mocking
laughter up on the range
as if she left the bloke
in the ute for dead.

It was a great wind-up
outside Yeperenye—
as if to say
Life's a joyous thing

with no maggots
in the middle.
Just wish I'd seen
her happy thunder face.

She had a loose
denim skirt, a dimpled
lumbar region—
buttocks that talked.

A man standing there
could but carry
his heart
strung around his neck.

Ready

High three-quarter moon
straight out of the icebox.

Drifting north
over the crawling, outgoing
sea-gathering sheen.

Arthur/Martha—
any man or woman within
gathers wits for indigo.

The last cormorant dives
comes up, preens in
cold shroud, flutter-rising.

As if she might be gone
from you already
or you from her
beforehand, any hand.

Imagination is premature
tidal race. In the present intervals
wear a Bardo nightcap
thank Buddha for her cats.

Pretend you're an old conifer.
Rise at the tongue of dawn
lap the world as water.

Turnips in Kyoto

Darkness in the eight-mat room

As the sun set in the hills over Arayashima you could hear chanting, probably from the grounds of the Imperial Villa. It comes from another world into this one, yet seems familiar.

That broken field of turnips
white and bluish after slaughter—
tops here, half-bodies there.

You walk up towards the tall bamboo
the sun setting cabbages
alight with silver.

What a mess—
the old ground of your thought
wounds and memories

straw brooms of good intentions
the all-too-familiar earth
the same, same self.

Cold Ears

Moon shadows tonight.
Wild boar in the woods
the deer with them.
No wonder the gardens are fenced.

Did the pigs do the turnips in?
Last night, when it felt like snow
was that a stag
watching over my sleep?

Downtown, the teens in tartan shorts
are watching 007.
It's Saturday night.
Up here not a dog barks.

My ears were cold
after the poetry reading.
Too much listening
to myself.

Over dinner
we talked of other poets.
The first dish steamed of the earth.
That made us feel heaps better.

Under the Carpet

The moon is on its back
or maybe its smooth belly.
It hangs both ways
as fully itself as a sword.
From Shugakuin the city lights
are fat, palatial slugs
aglow in slow time
a gentle carpet—
those civil wars swept under.
No sound. Only a cat
on heat in the tin shed
its natural siren carrying on
as I slope up the hill
past those hacked turnips.

Han Shan on the Bus

On the way back from Daitoko-ji
irked by instructional gardens
I read Han-shan on the bus
agreeing and aging with each word.

Each morning I see a lizard neck.
Each night bones commune with dust.
But still I hope for a pure heart.
The days here give a lucid dusk.

At Shugakuin the hills are a cradle
The moon a half lamp. I came
up by the clinic and school
a short cut through the shrine

in under its bracing gate.
A pine roped behind a red fence.
A bell hanging in the dark.
I was quick around it, then out

up between the frostbitten cabbages
unnameables under black plastic
that dug-field of turnips —
wounded torsos, loose white flesh.

Like the housewife ahead of me
groceries loaded each arm.
Soon I had the climb to myself.
All the craggy hermit said was true.

I reached my gate in the low wall.
Further up, perfectly pruned peach trees
stood spiky under the stars.
For the crystal night I had

Grass Hut Work (2016)

a wild piss beside the house
then went inside to forget the sutras
drink wine as rice steams. Truly
I don't know how old I am.

On Getting to Grips with the Heart Sutra

Surge plays on and off-key, mainly on. A gurgling wins over words,
                                            almost pings
dances down, pocks stone, thrums, flares in little hollows from time,
                                    like flames—

You sat by the door with the door closed and the rush was rush enough—
rain arrives and stays, is downpour, it wants the door closed, listen to its fall

as welcome as sleep is welcome, in far reaches of temples, it's touch cool
and still you are dry in the warm room, the rain sheets the glass, it's trying

to wash in, splashes back, onto the stone step, its gush, like your waking,
                                                is all there
all of the time now, dimpling and flooding, dimpling and filling the mind—

rain all night and now rain the whole morning, flooding the new morning,
                                                    making it
the old rain, time-worn, it falls as it always falls, emptying itself as it
                                        swells back up

gutters have all the time in the world, fat pebbled, grey stones grey as rain
light falling out of rain as drops, smooth stones, each drop loving stones,
                                            wasting themselves

the rain is all love of morning, having fallen all night, creeks, a river
it rushes on past out there, you can see it through the glass, the dark sheets

the morning's light yet to come right in, the rain to wash the day, you
if you'd let it, open your mouth, there's no roof, look up now, look up
                                            into the sky…

The sound of rain off wide eaves soothes the mind, the water fall, its force
the force in its gentleness off wide eaves sooths the mind, its outside-inside
                                            sounds falling…

Grass Hut Work (2016)

It gives vigour, it takes vigour away, it washes the mind.
The force of rain off wide eaves washes the mind.

Only the eaves, the eaves save the walls. Open the door if you dare!

On its slide, the door sound is avalanche. Fills the mind—with words, war.
What comes close is what you must have been waiting for, but who was
                                                                                       to know.

The ten thousand black horses ride on down from the sky over Hiei-san.
The ten thousand horses fall from their night into morning.

The water roar is grey-toned, silver flecked, black with a flame in it, wild

heavy, each streaming mane lead-heavy, thickening with downpour.

Hooves clatter on the stones, steam from their nostrils shoots into yours.
The clatter, the rumble out there! Its fox trot and stomp, the creature is
                                                                                       to be met.

If a breeze, the rain would whinny, hiss. As it is, there are the drops, the ten
thousand drops into the heart, the sound that beats inside and outside

the rain-sound that makes an eve for the mind (all these words)
the rain-sound that beats on the walls of the mind, eases it, needs

the mind to be inside it outside in the instant, at the same time.

Your welling up, a feeling of tears in the doorway, the heart wishing not
                                                                         to be hurt by rain
the body's alarm at the force of it all, the heat of its roar, its boiling ice.

Each drop has its outside sound, each drop breaks open from its centre
a catastrophe of walls crashing in, the empty sound splashing out—

and the running on of that, the spillage and joy of breakage.
Simple: rain-sound is celebration, of release, nothing more, nothing less.

No. The sound of rain tightens, its swells into itself, seizes its own notes
this way then that in its own race before bursting, there's more than one
$$\text{stream}$$

coming down, the light one that breaks—you catch, you think, its notes
and a dark one underneath, its pulse green and of the forest

it pushes the others about, but without reason, it holds some up, lets
$$\text{others go}$$
drives their shattering without reason, or without reason that you can grasp,
$$\text{the sound}$$

let in through the door your heart open
or as open as can be in a single morning woken by doves in the rain

the whole sound doubled and tripled by the percussive mystery and lack
of melody, or a melody that splatters here and there at your feet, threatening

to wet your socks, give you cold feet! Tempting it is to shut the door
keep the sound at bay, the roaring-cold-fire-sound you can barely fathom.

The door stays open. The sound remains a strangely terrible joyous
$$\text{sensation.}$$
It remains what it is, its drum in your throat, in the belly's pith

in the mind's eye, the ear's shell, it's in under the tongue that won't stop
wagging, jigging words on a string out there on the stone pebbles—

language does its dance in lovely runnels receiving rain
words dissolve out there, they wash back into the earth, leaving the sound

unfathomable. You keep sitting there like a voice-hearer—
those old timers who just wanted the lesson, the sutra straight, without
$$\text{rain—}$$

staying you, keeping you here, come to think of it, the one dry thought:
warmth arrives because you are inside it, warmth of the essence

the flow in warmth is the flow of something, as sure as a dove's call
the birds that woke you with their bubbly murmurs, their warm rain sounds.

The warmth's there as it empties itself like notes like drops
inside and outside at once, the sound crossing, re-crossing over—

thus speaking, you can say this, sound summonses the words
washing them in, words born, re-born in the pock of the mouth

and washed down, a body of water, words bound for the blood stream
words washed down incessantly, words for the gullet, vanishing into the
$$\text{runnels}\text{—}$$

running off eaves that keep walls of the mind standing
washed off eaves back into earth that mothers rain.

Rain, rain, falling inside its sound—rain-body, joy.
Rain, the rain, falling outside its sound—rain-body, joy.

All Over the Body, Hands and Eyes

You get to the old place at midnight
a three quarter moon burning high to the south
its heat wrapped in a smoky gauze.
The gate unlatched for you to bow
into your grass hut.

The bedroom gushes and hums.
The Otowa river roars in its race
a garden seethes with cicadas.
In the corner, a bed
under the window, paper screens

opening onto the sunken garden:
as if you might rest your head
in a forest clearing. Further up
in a millennial temple
a flame to peace still burns.

You scatter gear all over room.
Before nodding off in the heat
reading Dōgen's *The Issue at Hand*—
'flowers fall when we cling to them

and weeds only grow when we dislike them'.
The cicadas clatter their way
into the root of a skull.
You wake facing the bamboo
in the eastern window, waterfall-green.

Summer, and not a flower to be seen.
'When there is a single cataract in the eye
flowers in the sky show each way…
it is eyes throughout the body.'

Dōgen shimmers in bamboo.

At dusk, when cicadas resume—
metallic re-soundings in forest.
This morning, mid-morning and steamy already—
a continuous high-pitched hum
a high and low in unison, a stream of unbreakable

sound, vibrations arising from humid
ground and which hangs in the air
as agitation, assault
a rattling of weaponry.
No birdcall makes an impression on it.

You just have to start the day, face the music.

Unholy

One morning
    all these beginnings
        early enough to be fresh
            it was an awakening of sorts

you confessed to unholy
    satisfaction
        in the body by the fly-wire door:
        that it was dead.

Hanging there
    as if on a sticky thread
        on the grey matter
            of an old paling.

You marvelled at it, this flimsy
    proof of extinction
        so transparent
            in the light.
            A husk of violence.
            All that was left, say, of a spirited life.

A notation of the body—
    it had emptied itself out
        to become a remnant
            as empty of song
              if it was a song
    as life itself

            if life has a self.

Bashō's Sin

was leaving that kid
by the side
of the road.

Can some
larger Taoism
account for it?

'Hiroshima'—
pages in my mind
are peeling away.

I'll go there…
try to be naked, but
this ease of speech—

in summer downpours
the fatuous
'plum rain'.

I'll discover, I hope
the character
for my own shame.

The word for Peace
is made of Roof
over Woman

Another character
has the signs for Rice
and Mouth.

In the grass hut
I strive to be nobody
a hungry artist

albeit walking in
my old man's
peace-mongering steps

left left left
until I am hum
drummed and lost.

'We must be steadfast
to survive history'.
O yes yes yes.

Anyway, I'm afraid
of not feeling much
and of a word-rush
nonetheless—my after blast.

Truth is, if I am going
in good faith
it must knock me down
burn me through.

Rough Notes

A ghost just got on the bus.
His skin is paper
like a dead cicada.

Barely a body
apart from its trappings
their semblance of weight:

the umbrella, the black smock over his robe
the silk socks in which his toes
divide for the temple slip-ons.
And the feline handbag, from which he pulls
his sheet of tickets
tearing off two hundred yen's worth.

The train races south in the glare of sun…

You're swaying along recalling
Wilfred Burchett the Communist
who once so loved
the silver hulls of B29s.

His packed carriage rattled
with the samurai swords and daggers
of Japanese officers.

Do not smile for fear of seeming
to gloat at their surrender!
The sharing of fags lifted the mood.
A swig of sake
put everyone to rights.

Grass Hut Work (2016)

Almost Forgetting

Ogura writes—with a touch of shame—
of the bomb's 'monstrous magnificence'
the 'pageant of clouds' after the blast.

Surveying the city on the second day
'the sensation' was of 'looking down into a volcanic crater'
which was 'further advanced by the dark of night falling.'

The bright juxtaposition of the Milky Way
and the other stars in the night sky
with the fiery ruins below
gave such an impression
of 'primordial grandeur'

'it almost made me forget my worries about you'—
speaking of his wife and children.

Of mothers, he observes
dementia at the loss of their children.
For days in their arms they carry dead children.

Untitled

Think of your mother's puffy ankles
her skin peeling around them
like her old stockings.

Think of her being
a nanosecond from your dear self—
a black patch, in sticky tar…

When the peace crowd thins
you can go in search
of the *atomic shadow*.

Poor Reason

In Kawabata's exquisite, private collection—
a hand, by Rodin.

Here is 'the thinker'
incinerated on the steps of a bank.

His shadow is the thing.
A bleaching of thought—

the press of poor reason
into the quartz.

Boy O Boy

Oppie the live-wire.
Oppie the *Destroyer of Worlds.*

Oppie the Red, Oppie the Astro Boy
who predicted black holes. Mad Oppie
who left a poisoned apple for his rival.

Oppie who strutted his *High Noon.*
Oppie besotted at Point Zero
in love with *Trinity.*

Oppie and his numbers men.
'Ain't God Great'—
at the math that came out right.

And the top-secret news
reached Potsdam:
'The baby was born.'

Secretary of State Stimson
so happy he might have given
birth to it himself.

And Dwight slumped and said
the secret code said
'The lamb is born

or some damn thing like that'.
Back in the desert Oppie cried:
'Oh my, this is hard on the heart.'

'Now we are the sons of bitches'.

Like Grass

On the plaque of the monument
near the bridge with its contortions
simulating the suffering of steel
the writing is carved
into the marble—
'grass style'
beautifully light in gestural presence.

It tells of hair.
Hair lost at a snail's pace
compared to hair piled into a cabinet.
Hair lost over two weeks, say…

To some
the resemblance to a monk's tonsure
was striking. Then, as soon as fifty
days after the blast
it could grow again.

Crazy Iris

How the Humanist
—like Ibuse's 'crazy iris'—
springs up in one.

From the *Oriental Hotel*
you step out into Heiwa Avenue.
take a left into the shady lane
find it does not have the stench
of death, only the sky-high
pictures of girls
who will dance with you.

It's broiling heat, the same clutch
of words thrum in the skull.
You've heard that
today
for the first time in sixty years
The US Ambassador will arrive
at the Peace Park.

Even so
hundreds already stream
towards the fully grown, green trees
occupied with battalions
of cicadas.

Canopy upon canopy around the concourse.
You did not know the war had spared so many.
Every seat occupied, the ground littered
with veteran men and women
each with a time piece.

And then the long, green, humid wait.

Silence is suddenly upon us.
All of us.
Everyone standing with their hats off
heads bowed
to the toll of the bell.

A wild thought at 8.15:
Consider each cicada as a sentient being.

In the same instant birds ignited mid-air.
Mosquitos and flies, squirrels
family pets crackled
and were gone.

To Speak of Tragedy

That the speeches in the Peace Park
settled into the late morning
hum and husk-making
of cicadas, those survivors
making ashes of the mind.

Lines Found in My Father's Hiroshima Folder

Among his foolscap papers—
tucked into a report to the central committee
of the Metal Workers Union
there's a spectacular poem
printed in East Berlin
as bitter as Brecht
murderous of hope.

I rather think he'd be embarrassed now.
I bet that when he flew
from Tokyo to Hanoi
in 1972
from Peace-Conference to the B52s
he'd have forgotten about the poem

but once back home
he'd have pulled it out
to contemplate what no-one in the movement
could afford to say. He tried
as I try now to imagine the words
spoken by a woman, in her Japanese.

Ah yes, this year
I lack energy.
Peace! Peace!
I am tired of hearing about it.
I am exhausted with unreliability.
Disappearing into a deep sky, and
done in with fretfulness
unable to find the answer,
no matter how loud
I yell and cry.

I have become sick of everything.
The more uproarious the people,
the emptier my heart is…

Fukuda Sumako called her poem 'Talking to Myself'.

The Loveliest Things

were sighted earlier that morning
and later the same day.

Three spotless men escorting a trolly:
each conducting himself
preciously before and aft
keeping the sail cloth—

no, it could have been silk
draped over an object
as fat as an ox

which suddenly revealed
a part of its body as bronze
its lower lip as a bell.

Furthermore, at the last tolling
as the crowd dispersed
and the flowers, near the flame
rested in each other's arms

you looked across the concourse
saw the sliver of orange
heard the first beat

and the chant that belonged
to the monk who led the others
who held his fan, his drum
as an offering of notes

the drumming being the offering
the chanting being the peace-making
the line of saffron robes
a body as strong as an ox.

Grass Hut Work (2016)

Boy with a Pigeon 1944

In the palm of one hand
I can feel the soft weight of the bird
all its downiness of the kind
I had, once upon a time
on my cheek, my upper lip.

In my other hand its feathers quiver
then settle like a silk bow tie.

Blue sounds, blue sounds—
the bird colours my jacket
calls into my stiff throat.

Then we can't help but
bunch up a bit, tuck down
for a pin-pointed look.

Naked Clay: Drawing from Lucian Freud (2012)

Girl in Bed 1952

*But those who come are not even children with
the big indiscriminate eyes we had lost...*
             —W.H. Auden

A hair's breadth of ice
             blue in the pupil.

In leaning towards her
             she inclines to miniature.
You catch your breath. Too close.

She discriminates even as you glance
away, as if to say

come, go as you like
I am well in knowing damage.

She is terrifying interior Wedgwood—
of clay that once was mauled.

Naked Clay: Drawing from Lucian Freud (2012)

Narcissus 1950

*Sometimes when I've been staring too hard I've noticed that
I could see the circumference of my own eye*
                —Lucian Freud

What is it he sees?
Dove or dead monkey?

Or the still dreaming lilies
that are his hands ?

If he could he would lift his head
hear the blue calls.

As it is
the water's frozen, holds him there.

Would that he could thread
his pullover right through

recover the half of his head
cut off by the ice.

Sadly (he knows, he knows)
he is crowned by each dry hair.

Girl with White Dog 1950

The girl with the white dog
as still as the door closed behind her
is daydreaming of mice
in a drawer of socks.

As if summer has breezed
into her recess of room
she is cooling a full breast
as bare as an egg, pale as milk.

The other breast is in her gown.
With one tender hand
she supports it with the weight
of the head of the dog

that rests its muzzle on her leg.
The svelte grey hound is also pale, smooth
and perhaps like a cat
a lapper of milk.

The other hand is by her side
in line with the dog's head
the gold of the wedding ring
in tune with the ginger tints

of its nose, eyes, the inner ears
painted with a mind to bats,
and the dimple of the woman's throat—
the slightly moist parchment that listens

hears everything.
Smart the dog that nabs
the bend of the leg, the turn
that offers calf and thigh

Naked Clay: Drawing from Lucian Freud (2012)

the staunch hip under the downy gown
its plaited tassel dangling
from her lap to slightly parted knees
and the rest point of the dog's muzzle:

its muscular folds of flesh and bone—
like her shoulder and collarbone
like the planes of her lips and cheeks
their lustre of dried-out seashells

offsetting the glints and gleams:
on fingernails, nostrils, nipple
along the pod of a lower lip
in pupils, swimmy rims (the four of them).

Folds of its neck, folds of her gown.
Her arch of foot a swollen flipper.
A dog with the weight of a seal.
Their waters warm and rhyme.

Fathers and Daughters

1
And the bead curtain
with its chinks of revelation:
her eyes, bird's eggs
the manner of her mannerly
hands, wind chimes.
A father's blue hat
and matching cravat.
And between his knees
the little girl with her lovely
green felt coat
buttoned up with one button
her life barely begun.

In their doctor's surgery habitat
they are waiting:
the father's gaze is blue
the little girl is kitten bright
and rather sad
the fall of the beads their frame.

2
In the tenderness of evening—
the girl's white bow
a bird at rest on the promontory
of her shoulder.
She's gazing upward at a distant flock
her father might have shot as clay.

The air is alive with potential.
She, she feels, might one day fly.

He is sentinel to his fledgling
who will bear the weight of his dying.

Naked Clay: Drawing from Lucian Freud (2012)

Meanwhile their secret affinity lies
in the fragile flesh of the father
and the quiet pinks in her:
in that bare throat with his shirt collar open
hers high, turtle-dove grey.

Woman Smiling 1959

It's his 'amplifying the touch'
that gives her the wry smile
of the spring tide

as if light on the face
once fired
has eased the clay open
quizzically.

I imagine her finding
mariage à la mode
amusing, or her hotfooting
out the window as his lordship
steams in.

Either way she's free
as the Shrimp Girl
rosy and only herself to account for—
'society' almost tossed off.

Colours of a Breast (*Pregnant Girl* 1960)

Wind very brisk… clouds moving very fast…
  John Constable *Hampstead Notebooks,* 1822

Cream and pale green,
mauve and tangerine
the blues of slight bruises
rouge, pink, milky tea
ginger, lime, verdigris.

Strangely, there is nothing
entirely raw here. It is
nudity of colour in full dress.

It is a kind of slippery
symphony, or egg-shelled
chamber music –
the interior strings of mother
a drying breeze in the nursery.

With the fullness of weather
a firm study of clouds
over the swoon of the Heath
has been carried indoors.

Naked Child Laughing 1963

She's in a tizz of a huddle
as if a waterfall of mirth

splashes her body pale
with embarrassment.

Her shoulders, the smooth skin
of her arms, a bare breast—

flesh of cyclamens
the 'diva' flower the painter loves.

She's the painter's daughter, in fact
her body one long tending—

a girl with plump hands
her legs on a swing, thighs heroic

her limbs in the breeze
of a green bank.

She's a naked spirit
clothed in happiness

the gush of a fountain
held in her wide mouth.

And father has rendered
her eyes dark, teeth strong.

Naked Clay: Drawing from Lucian Freud (2012)

Man's Head (Self-Portrait) 1963

A smear of snotty cream
marks the forehead
for the squall. Cheekbone, chin
veer into the dock.

There is, long would there be
a vigour of shoulder. A killing
power. Beyond that
the alley is unlit.

Tousled the crown—
almost that of a tosser.
The eye, the green one
near the bruised ear

is slant
the other a dead black
slit for the scream
muted by the head's twist.

Naked Clay: Drawing from Lucian Freud (2012)

Mother: portraits

He would give back to the son the mother's richness of feeling
—W.H. Auden
In Memory of Sigmund Freud

As if her lips are sewn
        into a purse of silence
he gives back in tenderness
        the ferocity buried there.
In wisp and sliver of acid
        this is mother and metal
the final etching of one
        whose end is his new beginning.

In a painting the colours are made
for a Prussian afternoon
the winter tints set down
for a slow pounding:
he has settled her for a surveillance
of inconsolable care—
creased as the leather of an old chair.

Reading, all facets of her face
        incline to the page, its shadow.
But the page has been painted blank
        her hair the same grey—
with a touch of blue where print might be.
        Maybe, one day, it will come up braille
and she will finger the words
        touch their material essence
like the love letters girls once wrote
        to her dear talented boy.
As it is, he is letting her fall
        into a studio snooze.

Now she's on her back, paws up.
One soft palm shows like a pup's belly.

Long live the eiderdown and the paisley
garden on her dress and collarless vest.

Mother is adrift, the son intent on every thread.
Each dwells in the other's dumb eloquence.

Beige, the greys, the fawn pillow serve
to smooth the puff of throat, cheek, chin.

You can feel her settling, uninquiring
listening to the brush patterning her in, in.

A year has passed in the studio.
Her rest is grim in time's wood.
Gone is the sterile rail of the bed
like the one in my mother's hospital ward.

She's close to sleep, not quite absent
the jaw more of a square jaw.
Could she be losing her speech
as my mother lost hers?

The pillow's lush, her bed a touch satiny.
Indentations make a soft respite.
She has resolve, she lies in wait
one hand closed, the other raised

in a kind of farewell, the fingers half opening.
But she's not gone yet, she's too much of a piece:
her dun-coloured cell exquisite—
the embroidery there for embalming.

Naked Clay: Drawing from Lucian Freud (2012)

It *is* late; she's lying peaceful as a nun.
The white top, the white skirt, they complete her.
A jaundiced blind is drawn.

Beneath

Ineptitude consists in wanting to reach conclusions.
　　　　　—Flaubert to Louis Bouillhet, 1850

It's a large interior that throbs
with meaning, tests its own seams.

It holds, barely in order
two ungainly dreams.
The skirting boards do not meet.
No one is meant to speak.

It contains his mother's head
painted against a rough blanket—
her face beneath the bridge
of a younger woman's knees.

Mother is in a black chair.
The other, her son's lover
lies half-naked behind her
each adrift from the other.

If one has been quietly weeping
the other will not have seen.
The lover has made a grandmother
of Mother, and Mother might not know.

And there, under the chair
is a pestle and mortar
its weight like the spirit of a woman
set down after pounding.

The thick end is in the bowl.
The knob of the handle sticks out
over the bare boards of a floor
as boring as the blanket.

Naked Clay: Drawing from Lucian Freud (2012)

There is no cat on the mat.
The mortar could be a chamber pot.
Neither woman knows
exactly what is what. They dream

as the son the lover paints them.
His mother's mouth is firmly shut.
The lips of the lover are open
her nipples stiff, her breasts

level with the hair
the grey line of the mother's brow.
And as they dream the chair of one
intersects with the other's bed—

an unmade bed, its mattress bare.
And a torn chair, a rip
under one of Mother's hands.
The other's a claw, almost

that serves a dreamlike purpose:
it's the midpoint of painterly flesh
between the lover's lovely face
and Mother's nearest hand.

So there you are.
The son, a master of odd angles
has pulled it off. By a shitty blanket
two strangers are united

and much else besides—
each mysterious as the mix
of soft and hard, the mélange
of what is clear and what

can never be quite cleared up:
that other bulge, for instance—

Naked Clay: Drawing from Lucian Freud (2012)

of Mother's brown-stockinged
increasingly numb fluidy foot.

As swollen as a fig
her ankle is on a cruel par
with the pestle. The pressure of one
compounds the other.

Studio Songs

1.
No matter who they are, the paint
the skin of skins
is what counts.

Flesh is elastic, tinted and tuned
oiled for drying
is spring and welcome.

You thicken looking, you return to earth
the clay of the brow
is someone's touch.

It's a mess, a birth, a death—
your prime self
ready to fire.

2.
(life is) a mere spasm of consciousness between two voids.
       —Francis Bacon

Bring them in.
Let them be solid
in this sallow light.

Allow them safely ... *inside*.
Fathers and sons, wives, daughters
orphans of their time, the free ones.

See, they compose themselves
or have been composed
responding to a guiding hand.

Now they have fallen
into their freedom—
preferring to sleep.

No matter. We have them
here as we have perhaps
each other. Muzzles quieten.

3.

We have to be in a desert. For he whom we must love is absent.
　　　　　　　　—Simone Weil
　　　　　　　　Gravity and Grace

They dream an oasis
having come a long way
baked in an earlier light
to settle in a shade, of sorts.
No salt, a few wizened dates.

The desert we make of interiors—
a Sahara of lanes, canals
basements taking water
skylights leaking dusk
heartbreak tap-drips, cats piss.

The electricity in
the encampment is static.
Yes, some have a touch of the exotic
a few do dress-ups.
But the mirror is cracked
dance has left the belly.

The Roar, Reflection (Self-Portrait) 1985

This one has a different strength.
You are raw-boned
stronger and startled (not a bad thing).

The fox has settled into its lair
looks out at the risen sun.
There's an eagle somewhere.

What a shadow the head creates.
How our faces can spill into a torso.

Here is a man who will chop the wood.

And beneath the skin, the bone
there is a tree.

There are trees and there are trees
in this supple, subtle world.

Some stand in their rugs of bark.
You can hear them speaking.

Others look out
in their deceptive quiet
as a spring roars underground
surging upwards through them.

The lips of the timber-cutting man open a little.
He is watching himself listening.

Naked Clay: Drawing from Lucian Freud (2012)

Lying by the Rags 1989-90

Savagely she's been lowered
from a cross of rags
to be settled, if you can call it that
wide-eyed on the bare boards....

The chalk of the rags speaks
filth to the splenetic whites
in the grain of the boards
that seem to share

the knife-scrapings on her arms
throat, undersides of breasts
ribcage and hip bone plus
the white of the one eye

we can see is turned
to look along the floor
at some distant scene—
the crack under the door, perhaps

or the march of the boards.
But there's the aerial view
the limited naked terrain
of studio, battle ground, graveyard.

She's oddly laid out, at one with mess.
Her underarms sour, pelvic stubble
bristly as a lavatory brush
the rags brittle, metallic—

Paint saves her from dismemberment.

Eggs

Four eggs
as a matter of fact
on a plate.

Brownish
with some off-white
highlights

like flesh
on ribs
without the bruisy pinks.

Eggs meant
(their biscuity warmth)
for a soft palm

or Flora's
creamy pillow
her eyes open

the eggs
her lovely morning
understudy.

Naked Clay: Drawing from Lucian Freud (2012)

Esther 1982

In a moment when the cheek presses the pillow
a warmth returns to her face, heat in the bed rises
and the throat, with its extra lustre
informs mouth and summer lips.
The teeth, if glimpsed, might gleam with eye whites.

As it is with a filly in a stall.
When the afternoon draws to a close
the nostrils of a creature—
husband, lover, mother, father
sister sense the moist dark.

The manes we have want to be brushed hard.
A fine head feels heavier than a heart.

Painter Working, Reflection 1993

Lucian is wearing Vincent's boots.
(laceless however, the palette knife useless for ears).

The bed has been made for Munch.
(but there's no dressing gown, the disrobing's complete).

The shins of the painter could be out of a jinker.
That tilt of head—like a horse in a stall

except that it's being held for a mirror
that is inside, there's no figure more indoors

than this man without shame, a strong man
his muscles and bones are clods turned by a snowplough.

After a while you get the impression
he's painting himself inside out
he stands like a tramp
because his work's a trance, a ghost-dance, a rhyme into
        exfoliations, scrapings
          a whimper fills the mouth

the kind of thing we do when
we are more alone than we know, closer
to death than we think, when we don't
have to think about work or how we
        look anymore we just look
even as we leap…

An old man walks into the room, strips
stands strongly with his equipment
durable as the gold band Rembrandt
painted around his own throat.

Naked Clay: Drawing from Lucian Freud (2012)

And there is a touch of mystery
maybe even a late stage vanity.
That scabby looking foreskin, its impasto has
the rakish air of a thick felt hat.

Naked Man, Back View 1991-92

After he did the belly and loins, he turned Hercules around—
did the back, the shoulder of bare mountain
and the long slope down towards the valley.

Nothing untoward, however. No dogs either
no ballsiness of whippet, their snouts making kennels of rooms
the 'congregations of genitalia' warming mats, beds.

Just the bare slope of a man who could ape giving
birth to a world; this carried out under bright lights
in the faces of those who wouldn't couldn't dare

A gloss for his satiny skin. A sheen along the thigh.
The Sumo nape done understatedly. The skull's
indent tender as a fontanelle.

And the hammy foot, given its luxury of burgundy mat
a pile thicker than any other body had been offered
a royal elevation above the old bare boards.

A great man in a small throne room, in fact.
On a low stool as fleecy white as the Aegean in winter.
A talented Australian arse as warm as toast

Naked Clay: Drawing from Lucian Freud (2012)

Benefits Inspector Sleeping by the Lion Carpet 1996

Because I keep the company of lions
he's given me a Jack Dempsey nose.

I'm still in the submarine of sleep
but I'm dreaming savannah.

The lion roars above my head.
The she lion is just over my bare shoulder.

The claws are seeking their deer.
He attends to my fingers, my toes.

The poor deer, their startled flight—
beautifully dashing on the wall of my cave.

You think this primitive, my master's
irony cruel? Say what you like but I feel

woven into a temple.
What I have is what many want—

a shameless quiet, a wound that knows
the weight of sacrifice.

Daphne

The way the path goes down to the gate. Constable's so marvellous at that. You think there's nothing more moving than a muddy path going down to a gate. Tells you everything.
—Lucian Freud

Unless it is an elm.
Which he loved, and you failed.
Its impossible bark said go
go back to your bare boards.

There, under electric light—
forgetting sun dashed upon stones
those waterwheels—
you grow her thighs up from the floor.

You muddy her shinbones
her loins, their leaf-litter
make her belly caterpillar creamy
her heart-space chalky
let her strong arms, folded behind her
branch in their own rough ways.

Mottle her face
shade its downward gaze
under that thatch—
hard-dried looking, stiff as a haystack
out from which her dark pupils stare.

Now you're near the end of
the path.

Her torso, nippled and lovely erect
a copse of saplings packed into it.

Naked Clay: Drawing from Lucian Freud (2012)

The Painter Surprised by a Naked Admirer

as he damned well deserves to be
after all these ticky-tacky years
soiling and being soiled
leaded and unleaded, head heavy with Cremnitz
living the life of a prize smear
staying up half the night with rags…

What woman wouldn't go down—
be bare on the bare floor
sniffing his oily woodwork
keeping his thighs company
checking their health, their tree-stump
strength and protean quality?

Gallantly he pits her presence
against the mess he's made of wall
his fury of backdrop
their crib of a love nest
his gloriously free comic routine
and her bliss, there's no mistaking it.

Every other woman can go jump.
And the gormless feminist men, too.
Brave the fire that's in submission.
See how ignitable she is—
like that bundle of sticks on the stool.
Brushes, some say, but they're ready to burn.

He's even made a clearing in the room.
They could swing a dozen cats.
The wall, every stab and jet, ripples with mirth.
And what does he say about what
he's been doing with faces lately?
Those not hers—

I'm thinking of *Ria,* the golden one
a face that's pitted, ecstatically roughed
as if he'd break each atom open…
as with all naked admirers
who'll cling to what they must—

what's oily, hot, conflagrations of riposte.

from Magnanimity

…No light on the body
nothing to speak of, that is—no annunciation

hardly a shadow
just light in the paint becoming flesh.

Peaceful as death is said to be
as given as trust and blood.

Delicate. You half expect to see
a napkin of crumbs beside them.

They have partaken of the world—
here is their offering of themselves.

Shall we eat now?
Shall we set something for them?

Time breaks open at the table.

Thrush Summer (1959)

That bird, in the heat
bursting out of itself.

Yellow field, a harvest
in his song to the sun.

Young man bird
woman at his call—

the season springy
androgynous as apple sin.

Blake dreamed him.
Palmer nested him Christian.

Every cider press
revived him, danced him—

O summer thrush of youth
a rush of beaky songs

the streaming of bass notes
as if culture is new!

Conflagrations!
The corn under starry skies.

When we were young and ablaze—
spirit arrivals!

Lines for Birds, with the painter John Wolseley (2011)

Eagerly We Burn

From the war-zone of burnt goodbyes
    charcoaled bodies on the moor
        long shadows under warming skies
            with a cold southerly whipping the nape—
                we create.

And here, after the fires
    there's amber growth from tubers
        frisky ginger everywhere
            tiger tufts from earth, a tricky life
                those hakea have

disguising their spring. The reeds, too
    and the spear of the Black Boy
        its thrust of yellow flower is sweet
            making greedy bees of us
            plus all the virgin greens—rapacious.

At night, in ocean moonlight
    phosphorous gathers along the thickest trunks
        where out of armpits and pubescent
            breasts, in succulent scallops
            leaves from sudden juicy stems
                suck on the laurel morning.

And here comes Harlequin
    unfurling himself as paper
    Harlequin in Pierrot guise, prince of frottage and the breeze
            touching and rubbing and almost free
            as a breeze, if randomness is free.
    In this particled amorous air
        eagerly we burn.

Lines for Birds, with the painter John Wolseley (2011)

Paper as waterfall—tree-made, tree-born.
    How we scroll ourselves
    these shorter, later days after the blaze
        with the charred all around
            the things we thought gone
            exhaling, offering their scratchings.
            The page we are recovers the world.

Twiggy fingers, our bird marks
    the fields we are in, waves of retrieval
        the smudges we make of the abstract—
            a poor elegies for Plato—
        but around we go in new greens
                lettuce dances with Lao Tzu.

Haiku as fire song
    wilful syllables on one side of the banks
        whisper snowflakes on the other.
            Brevities of opposites on each side of the scroll
            make a singing space
            for a regal Honey Eater, look—

Flame has charred its back
    yet kept its yellow alight
        it's here but not really here
            in country badly creatively burnt.

If it perished it would live
    in the lines you make.
            Loves marks the time, we can print the world
            in dreams
                of white on white.
                    Eagerly we burn.

Lines for Birds, with the painter John Wolseley (2011)

Masked Woodswallows

They fluff and huddle—
a dark grey cap
a light grey cap
beaks ice-flow blue.
Snow cloud ancestors?

But here they are
with sweet *chap chaps*
in the warm sway of coolabahs.
And in the heart of the heart
of their patter
in dappled winter light—
they chatter off shadows.

One comes, as it must.
The little flat heads
jerk back, thorn-beaks open
point skywards
as the earth darkens
to the raggedy crossing
of the endangered

Red-tailed Black Cockatoos
that lands
above and indifferent
to the sleek ones—
    their raucous
    hurling of life
    into its high relief.

Lines for Birds, with the painter John Wolseley (2011)

War Music

Bunjil's whistle is thin and strong.
Starting so close to the sun—
notes feather the indigo.

Eagle wingspan of its call
is an invitation to dance—
paint the body with ochre

be reborn in the trance
of a long glide. With the calm
eye of the crater

it explodes downwards
falls upon small mammals
with ballistic precision.

A great rustle of wing
regathers each line of itself—
snapping the charcoal.

Lines for Birds, with the painter John Wolseley (2011)

Our Winter Desert

To install yourself
near a Bush Curlew's patch
wait till its scratchings join
a high-pitched wind across the plain
with the Willaroo calling its name.

To connect in this wide
burnt out place, fire tail
the clamourous finch to its new grass
spot the talons under the eagle's wing-span tilts
tune to its sun-spot whistle.

As you go out
to sense the river's ancient fat—
you have thickets of calls, billabongs of melody
dusty stretches of hum
downy throats of buried song

clay pans where they once belonged
with the quiver of birds
dancing and singing their heart's nest
men and birds in the same tracks
calling the seasons in a pulse of names

first names that were painted up
which fluttered and swayed
echoed sense and doubled back
with wedding-tongue clucks, clap sticks—
names that knew their homes

names that sounded in sand
recorded by wind and drifts of sand.
In the ground painting was the name

Lines for Birds, with the painter John Wolseley (2011)

and on the bodies, all feathered
that danced the name's beginning.

And now here, by a recording
machine in the winter desert—a Painted Snipe
exotically named in colonial light
with notes to be marked on a sonogram
its tracks cirrus, its song petrified.

What We Didn't See

We were in bed, lights out.
On the estuary—swans
with their heads tucked under.
Even the miners were quiet.

Then, out on the deck—
a clatter and scrape, the screech
of metal chairs knocked about:
a full-blooded injection into our dreams.

We must have sat up
looked at each yellow-eyed—
face disc to face disc, so to speak

as we realised the possum
so fond of your climbing rose, our vines—
the ravenous ringtail had gone for good.

The absence left us there, sitting up in bed.
I kissed you in the dark
our under-bellies softly feathered
like the Powerful Owls' that had left.

Now you grieve for the possum.
At 3 a.m. I get up again
wishing I'd seen
the owl's descent, its talons right in.

Horrible.
Its wing's top feather is a comb
the lowest one trails an edge—
almost downy, like a moth.

Lines for Birds, with the painter John Wolseley (2011)

Truth

My wits find water in the trackless waste.
           The Hoopoe in *The Conference of the Birds,* Attar

Honestly, around here
in this swampy gathering
I expected to see the Hoopoe—
its crest a swam of honey bees
its silly look a form of wisdom
the swerve of its beak an open invitation—

But to what, exactly?
Who in deserts made by man would know?

Water, water
you can hear the Hoopoe call—
water needs to flow like natural goodness
or else we lose our Way.

Anyone listening?

The Warm Far North

The Godwits were meatier eating
than slaughtered Snipe.

As if they came back to the mudflats to rust—
their feathers dry blood as they fattened.

The shooters were smug— a brace about their necks
another from where they held their guns.

But Linnaeus's 'haemastica' (blood)
was for the breeding plumage, not the hunt.

Anyway, once plump, they were gone
up into the wind-lanes of the gods.

Think of them there as chestnut, ripe ginger.
If they were not so intent on the tundra

they might have flown out of kilns
hurled into heavens as a solid V.

Even having arrived
at the other end of the blue world

among ice-wind and hawk-eye
it's the downy brown of the male

its rufous baked breast
the foxy assembly of earth colours

that makes most sense.
Nesting in the straw marsh

Lines for Birds, with the painter John Wolseley (2011)

its black lichen like burnt country
in the prickly mix of a safe tapestry

you can hardly see what's up
or what's down in orange-yellow.

Gannets

They departed, the gods, on the day of the strange tide.
    —John Banville, *The Sea*

Of a gannet I could say—
like Ian Thorpe on the blocks
like a Porsche outside the club.

Sheer finesse is the thing.
But the gannet is more serious than that.
It is grave presence.

Gannets gives off ceremony.
As a congregation
they exude license.

I know, I live almost
as near to them
as I must to myself.

They propagate at *Pope's Eye*
just out in the bay: too far to swim—
approachable by small boat.

From a distance, the rookery is foamy chop
all frisky innocence, like a flock of nuns
their habits dove-toned, crossing St Peter's Square.

Closer in, you get the foul whiff of rocks.
Bobbing within a stone's throw of the mess
gannet pong hits you with the force

of decaying, de-frocked priests
bodies snow-white, their nakedness gross
powers stripped of merit, all terribly free.

Lines for Birds, with the painter John Wolseley (2011)

Gannets strut, they preen—'We are still the best.'
If they have a God, it's put extra time into the arrowhead
beak, a streamlined weapon that owns the head.

The eye is bevelled in black stripes to the beak.
Flat caps soften us up with pale mustard—
yellow hinting at ravenous.

The mystery is, the closer you look at the single-pointed
hungry ones, the more they seem identical—
an aspect of swarm, like lice.

Their grades of white save them, give pleasure
to the eye like a nautilus shell
like marble, like a stick of clean chalk.

And their flight, their flight when they take off
straight up, each bird is pure unto itself, like nothing else.
High in the heavens, it is a monastery of one.

The arrow becomes a kite
as one hangs, hawkish over the South Channel.
It's deep out there.

The sea is mackerel.
The penitent is homicidal.
The plummet is what it's made for

its white power marvellous with death.
If you're sitting in a safe boat
a resurrection looks credible:

the gannet reappears in the chop.
For an instant, a hopelessly heavy shag—
then soaring to do beautiful damage again.

Lines for Birds, with the painter John Wolseley (2011)

On the Brilliant Engagement of Two Paradise Riflebirds

Once in the thickening canopy
into which silk night had fallen
        I heard her rustle
        imagined the panels of green

and the blues, multiple blues
brushing against each other in a shimmer
        as if, in the dark
        we were joining kimonos.

What we did was preen and groom
our feathers. We opened the orange
        depths of our beaks
        pleased at the split husks

the crimson fruit, its surrender.
  We did not make the modern mistake
        of thinking ourselves ravens.
        We just hung, swayed

        in the whip-crack of morning
                athletically embracing emerald.

Lines for Birds, with the painter John Wolseley (2011)

The Feast

As birds are flying flowers
why don't leaves sing?

Messiaen heard a slow note
in the Iris. What sweetness

these leaves could paint
in the jungle air.

The desired bloom for today
is the Chestnut-crowned Laughingthrush.

Our guide sang
'Laughingthrush Laughingthrush everywhere!'.

Figs are closing ranks
ferns withholding tunes…

The other flower
is the Silver-eared Mesia

with its blackberry collar
that frills the bowl.

First glimpse
and you draw breath

before it pours into the mind
filling it like cognac in crystal.

Vow: 3 a.m.

Since birds are flowers
        we had best tend them
        garden their surrounds

singly they found their niche here
        in time and in space
        their calls become us

as memory
        at night, the trees are thick
        with sleeping birds

at daybreak
  we rise with them—
  downpours of recollection

each note a petalled thing
        half known by heart
        half known by heart

Lines for Birds, with the painter John Wolseley (2011)

Space Travel

1.

The one that keeps carving its way
through the air to this Bottle-brush Tree

making waves in the air
a flight path in mercury

its push into the atmosphere
too quick to see

but its trajectory so firm, deft
the air gets sluggish around it.

The long tail flattens the wake
leaving no trace to speak of—

only this sense of arrival
beautifully shaped and hard-won

as we once felt about space travel
or miracles

many shouted for joy
others held off naming—

so with the bird now in mind
the one that came this morning.

Lines for Birds, with the painter John Wolseley (2011)

2.

Now I have a name—handed down
by a person of ornithological note.

I write it as if it's just been said.
But 'Long-tailed Sibia' means little to me

except for its tail and the way it swings
between and above and below

bottled nectar like the bees
the tail white-tipped on a hover

then the whole of it settles
to raid the long moment.

How many visits did it make?
I lost count. I will say countless.

Yes, I now possess its slick name
but in a furious blur

of heart-beats in space
it stays anonymous.

Lines for Birds, with the painter John Wolseley (2011)

The Wave

We are all our lifetime reading the copious sense of this first of forms.
Ralph Waldo Emerson, Circles

They are a shoal
a karmic swirl
eating on the wing
creating new lives for insects.

They act like Communists
but they are individuals
with names out doing each other:

Gold Babbler
     Green Magpie
          Grey Cuckoo Shrike
               Spider Hunter
                    Verditer Flycatcher
                        Orange-bellied Leafbird
                    Black-throated Sunbird
          Long-tailed Sibia
Silver-eared Mesia—

yet all of a piece
     en masse
               in their hunting wave.

They drive their feast forward like plankton
     no fixture in nature
the whole flock having
a whale of a time
     fluid and volatile.

You can stand in the forest
        see them coming from a distance
            closing the space
            some ahead of themselves.

Lines for Birds, with the painter John Wolseley (2011)

> *The steps are actions*
> *the new prospect is power…*

as the Minivets this morning
were first in the turn—
crimson, cadmium
male, female…

> *The same law of eternal procession*

each breast with its light on
twittering and eating
passing overhead
the gnats unseen, killed, reborn.

You didn't see the Minivet's 'grey chin'
so much as sense its glee of unison
the vibrations in the wheel
    the eternal generator
        the hungry passing.

> *The way of life is wonderful;*
> *it is by abandonment.*

Lines for Birds, with the painter John Wolseley (2011)

Redstart

…des légions de Rougequeues survolent le Sahara…
        —Paul Géroudet, *Les Passereaux*

Birds invite us to gather together what it is we want
    when what we want
    is acceptance.
    Desire is simply
    presence of bird.

So a bird appears, like this redstart, with its frail hauteur.
    The heart says
    time and again
    wait here peacefully
    for the bird
    and it will come.

When it keenly looks, consider how your insect mind
    really wants
    to know
    all about the bird.
        Ask:
        what harm can
        knowledge bring?

Don't preen at what you think you already know.
    The perch
    for you both
    is the thing.
    Bare the sharp
    line of your throat.

Sit quietly and see what you might sing for the bird.
    Forgive his
    'cris d'alarme'.
    Welcome your

Lines for Birds, with the painter John Wolseley (2011)

  tiny, wild beloved—
  in from the desert.

Whenever in doubt of your own beautiful strength
  say it in French.
  'Pourtant,
  son naturel timide…
  sans abdiquer
  toute sauvagerie.'

Burning Eggs

Les Bouvreuils sont nés pour la neige.
Bullfinches are born for the snow.

You can hear their warm hearts
beating off the cold. They fluff like embers.

Some think they hatch the colour crimson—
a scattering of burning eggs.

Ils tirent vanité de leur courte vie.
They flaunt their short lives.

Passion

Birds are feathered with rhyme, their wings layered with notes (their tails less so).

The harmonics of feathers, the vanes we preen, are as good as song.

They spread their wings, as if they are showing the world their repertoire.

Their flight is a song, or the beginnings of one.

In the old days they had scales—only the wind we'd hear, a hiss over stone.

The coverts are ABABAB, tight angles for a feather in air (their tails for a looser rhyme).

Feathers arrived to warm their bodies with song. Or for flight, or for both.

The technical term is endothermic. Self-warming we are, like the birds.

But it could be ectosonic. Feathers, all their African tints, percuss the rhyme.

To an out-going metric, feathers conduct the band, to a sea as wide as the sky.

And didn't you know that *iro*, Japanese for 'colour', doubles for *sexy*, offers a syllogism:

A singing bird is flight, is music of feather for love. As poets we preen for a rhyme.

As poets we peck at the metrics,—all those solo syllable counts— pure flight.

Like pure flight or a brilliant billabong measure for the unruffled
    Magpie Lark—

the bird that plays the intervals, the intervals, one feather at a time.

Or think of bird as featherless, needing no rhyme, calling up its
    nakedness.

Messiaen's Music for the Reed Warbler in the Sologne marshes at night

1
Tinklebell, tinklebell—
>ice keys in a hedge
>frost notes on a pond.

La Rousserolle effarvatte's
>notes
>bloom in the dark

the bird's all nerves—
>sets of light fidgets
>runnels in sword-sharp rushes.

And gently in frogspawn
>the notes spread
>foam into melody
>>for night fall.

And everything's upright, in silence
>in the perfect unison
>of silence.

All you can hear is the mauve of water lilies
>and yellow iris
>>ready for sunrise.

2
'…a blackbird duets joyfully with a Red-backed Shrike. A chuckling solo for the Redstart. The chords of sunrise intensify… a medley of incisive calls: the raucous Pheasant, the Reed Bunting, weird laughter of the Green Woodpecker, the whistling glissando

Lines for Birds, with the painter John Wolseley (2011)

of the Starling, the Great Tit, nervous fluttering of White Wagtail (exquisite in its garb of half mourning).'

3
Light dapples
        water flows about lilies
        notes ripple in bronze, in greens
        delicacy is paper-thin glass—

childhood memories
        come apart in the hand
        but no cuts, no bleeding—
        tissues of glass
        just—
micro tinkles
each note a glint

you can make a shower, cascades—
a glissando of departures
before tinklebell
belltinkle
on its new edge

everything vertical for silence again…

5
And the scythe:
        one sweep, the master cuts
                the notes free
                they swell as they fall—

sheaves of startlingly fresh sound
        peeps that cave into

    chords
    the throats of warblers
    deep as our own

as we stand in the morning air
   enjoying the breeze
     fecund tints
     swamp in the nostrils—

the notes that fall into the well
   of sound—
      sound to be trusted
      once and for all
      if you catch the form.

6
And the measure returns:
   all heart, full of feeling
   you can wear la Rousserolle on your sleeve
       but then—
    gone again

the tune fallen apart
   the master piano pounds the song
   could crush the bird
     but the slow notes, their lowing,
       the creamy half tones
work their way
back into the hedge
   redo the shape

Lines for Birds, with the painter John Wolseley (2011)

of warbling
and the bird rests there
>   warm among twigs—
>   new twilight.

7
Cascades—
>   countless footprints
>   in the air
>   seed sounds
>   scatter in wild wind.

Notes splinter, darken
>   regroup in a late shaft of sunlight
>   melody flutters
>   in the undersides of reeds—
>   is lost again…

Later (how long how long?)
>   they recoup
>   as forms on stone.

8
Another waiting:
>   la Rousserolle unfolding her song
>   as patience itself.
You have to stay with each note
>   know painfully they've
>   divorced each other
>   in space
>   that   has
>   no   shape…

Lines for Birds, with the painter John Wolseley (2011)

9
The return comes across quick waters…
    A thin tune plays
    the reeds
    each blade sharp, sharper…

And the soft wood chips—
    vibrations, like insects;
    any tick now la Rousserolle will sing
    to dragonfly wings or

she will hop to the side
    surrender to the insect trill
        of Grasshopper Warbler, yes

another lull between ticks
    that fall off twigs
    into a chasm.

The interval can be an
    unbearable
    stake in the heart.

How to withstand
    the next attack
        of silence, that false
    sense of union
the master's wicked lopping

as he lets all the notes go again:
    atoms glossy
    hard notes with a green aura
    the melody a smear in the air

then all the old tinkling
a tune on razor blades.

Lines for Birds, with the painter John Wolseley (2011)

13
Later, much later still
>　half tones recoup the sky
>　*calm in down.*

(Where's la Rousserolle now?
>　What kind of goose-chase
>　is this?)

Klung Klung
>　the tune won't quite
>　go in the head.

O the eggshells we step on
>　O specked half-notes—
>　being hatched again.

Every note's a lure.

Kite / *Tobi*

In its turning circle you don't see the 'black ears'
any more than you see the whiskers of a rat in water.

In profile, on the bare branch of a tree, up towards the hill temples
you spot the beak, the useful hook of a garbage collector.

When it's overhead you don't think 'black'
not even at dusk. You see the lovely pale donkey brown.

And its flight is as soft—downy.
Silence spreads itself over the gurgling river.

Except for that moment near the bridge at Sanjo-Dori.
Mid-sky mid-river mid your contemplative walk

wings flap-snapped open like a spinnaker
an attack on your face, then the sound was behind it diving.

After that nothing. It was swallowed by night.
You would never know the story of it golden—

its flying arrival in light for the first Emperor
the blinding of enemies, its war service.

Lines for Birds, with the painter John Wolseley (2011)

Raven City

Though not solid saffron
they are the aerial equivalent
of taxis with their horns on.

By the satiny pool at the *Oberoi*
they sip aqua
hop between croissant crumbs.

Over at the *Fairlawn*
where the table's set with doilies
they cloud fig trees and pester
rats in the rockeries.

At dusk, when the cricketers
withdraw from the Maidan
they pick and dance in garbage
beating the kids to it
hopping on one leg, neck twisted
just to make the point.

Under the Sign of Necessity

For Nabaneeta Dev Sen

In the comfortable room, our bellies full
we had been talking ideas, of language,
and you had read a poem
the one about your young men hardened
by killing in the name
not of their mother, but justice.
And I had read a poem in return
one about the bomber with the pretty smile
and teeth like Mack the Knife;
and my wife sang a song
the one about tribal law and turtles.

Finally (except there's no finally)
your 'household friend' came in
and sat like an Inca with her shawl
which lifted like clouds from a mountain
when she sang those long notes
that fluted from valley to valley
yearning for each peak…

After the loving silence we all then had for each other
I happened to remove myself to the bathroom
from where, in the smouldering street light below
a near naked man washed at the pump
he gutter startlingly clean all around him
his body as fresh as the speech
he directed like water to a man nearby.

The listener had a small towel over his shoulder.
He seemed to have all the time in the world…
A song must have linked the rickshaw men.

Four Lines East (2009)

But then I had to turn away—
Neither knowing their poem
Nor the wars they might be in.

from At Varanasi

Day-by-Day Dust

How is it that the light
Blesses the dust?
What became of the world
That the dust is blest?
In the morning, before the sun rises
Pollen is heavy with dust.
This afternoon, driving back from Sarnath
Even *Hero Hondas* sweeten the dust.
As for that cow at the intersection
Her good cud is dust.
The mounds of green chillies shine
As if they are clear of dust.
No dust befalls the charm shop.

A New Great Day

The Pepsi girl has Bollywood breasts
And a pesticide kiss.
She's more deadly than Kali.
But I am outward bound
On this spring morning
Crossing the Old Trunk Road.
In the dusty white *Ambassador.*
The driver, who loves Hanuman
Plays tabla with his new horn.
With three monkeys on the dash
And a white marble lingam in my dilly
All is well with the river.

Time Traffic

Infrequently, but often enough to feel stellar
the power fails, the lights over the table go out
but before you can set candles they are on again.
No one seems to mind, it is taken for granted
in the way you might take a slow blink for granted
when you are trying to keep, say, a cow in focus,
after the dusty mother has paused at a new angle,
her horns at the edge of the embankment, her udder
close to the *Hero Hondas* as they dart about her,
her casual droppings steaming in the wake of diesel,
that sooty know-all exhaust from the old *Ambassadors*.

Thus you make your simple way in Varanasi
in and out of your own disorders.
Lights go on and off of their own accord,
a flood in you one minute a short-circuit the next,
milk flowing in you, blood mixed in it the next--
a strange time zone, it has drought, it has monsoon,
rough winds pick you up and dump you
on a wide sandbank with low water mid-river.
What calamity, such abandonment!
Such strange dislocating happiness!

The quick brown waters swirl, encircle.
The current is a mother's dreaming murmur.
From this spot in a good flood you will be picked up,
swept along in the chattery mud. Meanwhile
you have a tent, a small one with long pegs.
And a cooking pot, rice, a sutra.

Four Lines East (2009)

Himalayan Fire

As you casually entered the gompa—
Travel weary, a meagre warmth in you,
Too much mist in the lungs
The winter sun hit the sutras.

The mountain light, having raised the black frost
Shafted the night wind south
Raided the cave
Struck the west wall.

The ten thousand leaves slept in their boxes.
Their hundred thousand sounds
Were wrapped in saffron.
The scrolls were as separate as toffees.

Then, with the wall as good as on fire
And every box glowing like an old coal
You could hear the seed syllables
Crackling away inside you.

Darjeeling

At Chiang Mai with the Diamond Sutra

1. Four Lines

Each morning when you wake—
fisherman by the green lake.
Still rows on the mud bank
their lines in. What's the reality?

Their plastic buckets, knives
the stools, chairs, mats
the lime-yellow reflection
of the lime-yellow brolly?

Their early arrival
the jobs in town they lack
their patience in rain
their mastery of the squat?

Today, something is missing.
Your view of the mountain
that keeps you from Burma
where the Sangha are punished.

And the smear of the bank
is like the filthy ponds in India.
But this is not there, it's here
by waters with a possible raft.

It's not appeared this morning.
No raft as yet on the lake—
just the idea of it as you wait
fisherman's lines in mind.

2. Noodles

The trouble is you don't believe
you have it in you.
You take pause and weeds
not-nothing have returned.

You get glimpses but
concepts are your shattered screen.
'No self no soul no being no life.'
Mind darkens.

It's all effort—
incessant scratchings.
(even with a love song
you hear only words.)

A nagging apprehension:
of sun-bleached bamboo slats
the steps down—
so thin they give way...

Yesterday, walking by the lake:
fear of falling in. Yet
there you'd simply be—in
and closer to a dharma raft!

There's one row
safe on the mountain's mirror
its rickety planks held together
by tarps, frayed rope.

In a blue sweater, pants maroon
like Tibetan robes
the man stands with a golden net
hauling it up like noodles.

Four Lines East (2009)

Green River (at Ponte Garibaldi)

The genius of squares
their mastery of welcome
and respect—then
you come to the old green river
once stuffed almost as a sausage is stuffed
with potshards or corpses
it hardly matters…

but that it should still be so green:
a meadow of sweet basil crushed by condottieri
could not make it greener
its reedy edge
a peppery flow with the foam a wine gets
quickly poured downstream
a chest-plate cataract at the bend
you could tip yourself over the high wall or be tipped…
another dash of green girdles the hospital island
some waters are healing —
those boys in their red singlets
found their way down to fish in the motion
Reeboks among the reeds
rucksacks dropped like underwear
they lean and bend, lime-fingered —
innocent look that nothing happened here
nothing green remembers.

Crossing St Peter's Square
After Seeing *The Torso Belvedere*

Crystal the air   moving between
and around the columns
                                   there is no other body
every body is itself   for this opening
released to the square   just you and me

now you know how

                                   we were carved

for this cold air
I can see everything in the distance now
I was so close   you
make the light   and shade
how solid we are in   space
we were freed   from stone
the columns go ahead of us   beautifully
and the entablature   my once heavy thoughts
carry our images   around to each other
you who helped   make me
you who found me   in full happy stride

The stone curves and swells in the middle
above and around   in between
Have you ever felt so emergent and in between?

There's no choice   but to walk here
take the shape   of yourself in
under the clean   bowl of sky

winter light clarifies   leads you on
you have been chiselled   modelled
outside   inside

As We Draw Ourselves (2008)

I see you crossing the square
each cobble making thin			leather of your shoes
feet as bare as stone

				touch me anywhere

deep inside myself			the part you found
the shape you fixed on crossing the square towards me
deep inside my hard			moulded self
my rough edges				feel warm
these columns
walk me towards myself			towards you
					making a procession
near water				dashing fountain

As We Draw Ourselves (2008)

Disegno for Michelangelo

D'un oggetto leggiadro e pellegrino d'un fonte di pietà nasce 'l mie male
(Out of something lovely and rare from a fountain of mercy my suffering
is born)
—Michelangelo (lines on the back of a sketch for the Medici tomb).

Il Divino's early lines

Near the *disegno* for a capital, below its leaves
he has written part of a sonnet in a perfect and
almost flowery hand. It sits like a score, a set of strings
and the lines it makes, the fretwork, step into the mind

as strongly as columns in a piazza. His little song lives outdoors
even though, on another sheet, near a putto, an upward-reaching
naked man and a singular muscular leg, he writes,
Sol io ardendo all' ombra mi rimango

I alone remain burning in shadow.
I alone remain burning in the shadows my body makes.
I alone in love, for love, in the body of my shadows.

Turning them to light, enabling them, bringing their weight
into speech, making the rough day promise the slave freedom—
making the man his model his virgin his child.

If I die burning/Merciful fountain

If I die burning—wish for the flames to rise, as they will.
S'ardendo moro, and hear the *pietose fonte*, merciful fountain.
Fruit of the earth on fire, the waters boiling—rough beauty.
The spill of things across the stone, life and death in the piazza—

the fire and blood and damned water of our bodies.
L'amor mi prende e la belta mi lega
Love seizes me, beauty binds me. *S'ardendo moro*
the birds swarm in the piazza, dreaming of sea.

In the open air beauty, my enemy, swells with pride.
S'ardendo moro, I die flooded, *pietose fonte*
everything dashing. A heart of stone won't keep things in.

I die burning, here by the merciful fountain, *pietose fonte.*
Twisting and rising my pounding body illuminates the river.
Each to his own, hammered out by fire. *Al concetto.*

Cage

Only with fire can the smith shape iron
from conception into clear and fine work

Al concetto. From the conception—forms.
One is born with an acorn on the tongue.
The trunk is a given, the branches are our own.
Forests are burnt for the forge—a hammer, the chisel.

Hack through woods to reach the mountain.
Bite the coin, suck the pebble as you appraise the cliff's
face, the cheek bone to be quarried, a hip like your own.
His heart tested the axles of the cart.

A block rests in a man's quiet garden
pretending to be a dead weight. Nothing breathes until you fondle it
as you fondle yourself. The miracle is the transformation

of mass: to think in stone for flesh,
and then, as if gravity is sin, to make of the spine a willow,
of the torso, a cage—singing and still burning.

Model of a River God

My eyes, greedy for every marvellous thing

Water and stone give the true form, the line
of river, alchemy hauled from the mountain.
The torso in its full strong confessional—
languid from girder to casement, the soul

in its breathing shell *alma anima*.
Anima shaped to lie at the tomb's base
companion to *Night*, consort to *Day*.
The great river to roar beneath them.

But here it is terracotta and oaken
wood and wool, a luscious clayey preparation
for stone, the belly rippling like a salmon bed.

A god as open to native air as Giuliano
above with chest plate bare, his flesh emergent
from metal and leather like an offered breast.

Conch

Every lovely aching body is a conch for life
with death blowing through. The heart
a trumpet, the mind a flute, the belly a harp.
Torsos, which can be flayed with certitude

are trees of life, they branch to the sun.
The bare shoulders of a man heave virtue.
His loins, timidly great, await the moon
and stars to light the path into the wood.

Some are longbows gathering for war.
The quiver we carry for them is full.
At a glance, torsos twist and shoot straight.

Their force inhabits the air with eagles.
In the square the fountains are oceanic.
A body can fill time and space like a lion.

Legs Known Musically Are Drawn

Sweetly placed over four anatomical legs
with a madrigal number of lines to a thigh
Sotto duo bella ciglia
La forza Amor ripiglia

Beneath two beautiful brows
Love recovers its strength.
The gourd of each muscle a base clef.
The calf of each leg in full rhyme.

It's a page for thoroughbreds.
The race of life runs in it, breath steams
in the lines. For what poem should stable a man?

Regarding the thighs, each muscle is thrillingly
marked. It's hard to tell if, after the flaying, they signal God's
knowledge, or are set down in joy at each note. Or both.

At Assisi

O you that follow in light cockle-shells,
For the song's sake…
        —Dante, *Paradise,* Canto 11

Giotto

1
Feet, birds, hands
Two hands wide under blue hills
White bird in flight
Descending to halo and tree
A tree for the birds below
Sackcloth and white birds
Alert to hands, tree, halo

2
Heavenly plaster, celestial blues
Renders stars for sea-sky
Coral for love's reef
The story sails under tender spinnakers
Bare feet on forgiving decks
Each shape solid, soaring
Maps for the birds

3
Lullaby brings the boat in
Lullaby buoys her, berths her
Maps for birds, for wolves
Paws for all weather, stories
Come up in our faces,
Lamps, eyes to speak truth
Wind comes round for the good

4
We are frescoed and alive
As good as dead for the walls
The poor with us, simple
Talkative, stories for all weathers
Good as dead in truth
Space to blue space
The devils in their place

San. Damiano

Cup your hand
Rest it underground

Lie down
Carve the cave
To suit your belly

Let the curve
Of your brow
Your neck
Your open mouth
Tunnel the ceiling

At the end
Of the vault
Pluck out your eye

Put a cross
In its socket.
Rest.

Paint the walls
Of your inner gaze
Grow old

Be silent
Eat.

Your feet
Let your feet
Be bare on the stone
Let them smooth time.
Rest and eat less.
Pray.

Homecoming

You land with gold over the Red Centre still in your head.
The road taking you home to the sea is a lizard flattened in the heat.
The light does the talking, the light splinters all over the place.

Who lives here? Who comes into the leaf-lit room?
An ancient traveller is led by a warm lovely hand into a garden.
Look, look, look, says blessedness, before he eats and sleeps.

One bird then another bird keeps him afloat and awake—
lilypond mind, the lapping of silence, old waters that are deep,
a sleep at the bottom of the ocean, sleep drowning memory.

Later the same day that is night he wakes into silence.
There, nearby and faraway are the loved ones speaking,
the right words in their throat, cooing into his speechlessness.

Later the same day it seems to be the real sea he is in,
salting the odd word, washing him back into blazes of time.
Rediscovering his freestyle under the Turneresque bushfire sky

he swims--that's it you swam into the aesthetic of homecoming!
They have not changed they are only more beautiful your loved ones.
You kiss the return, you find specs of ash on the pillow.

Reading on the Darkening Plain

for Rai Gaita

In the dusk of the plains
he held his hands together palms up
each open hand the page of the book—
'I would read until there was no more light.'

Then he'd leave the veranda
go inside to light the lamp
breathe the fumes of kerosene
that singey smell that was weak heat

and light for the reading and waiting.
Eventually, across the plains, he heard
the crackling of the motorbike.
The father's head down over the handlebars

the son's still over one last page
on the road to truth … Then the soup.
Night closed in. The dog warmed him.
Outside, the moon, mother of clouds, drifted.

Now, a father, a husband
he dwells on the plains once more
reading among boulders—
books as solid as deeds, good as stone.

His house is beautifully lit
inside and out. A wood fire roars.
Under the moonless sky of the stone country
one word virtuously contests the other—

the other word, the lunar one,
sails in under the bedclothes,
reconnecting the sentences of the day.
The latest book cracks along its spine.

Sex in Japan

Are you writing the same poem
or just getting older
forgetting the details?

Your journey out began here:
in a *ryōkan* in Nikko
fucking your first wife
learning about deceptively
comfortable mats, love
obligation and ritual
your own paper-thin walls.

From *Hiroshima Mon Amour*
to *In the Realm of the Senses*.
After three wives you might know
the extent to which a man
can castrate himself.
Maybe.

That was then. Now?

You're back in Kyoto
remembering that python
an ample middle-aged tart
looped about her belly and thigh.
Her grinning cavernous show
had a row of Japanese men
leaning forward in unison.

You were not that much
more than a boy.
Now it's girls, girls
a paedo paradise.
They fill the mags

like pastel-coloured sweets
a damp patch to each wrapping.
Kawabata, eat your heart out.

I don't understand.
The elderly women are beautiful.
And I can't keep my eyes off those
lacquered reds wed to black —
the bowls, the luscious almost nauseatingly
scarlet or vermilion serving trays
and that blood-red teapot
with its silly long thin spout.

Dojo

The teacher has a scoop of a face, like a sliced melon. He is quick to welcome: a student finds a chair, set, you later realise, under the lustrous poster of the young man who is the teacher's pupil, now the All-Japan Champion delivering a mawashi-geri with the ease of a leopard stretching. The sole of his striking foot is soft/hard, and higher than his head. It's a regular class.

No one's perfect in the warm-up.
Every body has cold hamstrings
a groin to care for, fine ankles.

Everyone can count the ten thousand
kicks and punches in their sleep.
Forms dream them.

Forms take them by the flying hand.
Forms marry their dance with respect
with death.

Sweat sweetens intent
and the snap of Sensei's ghi.
A monk ties his sleeves back

for the day's chores;
Sensei lets them be
in furious feather of pointedness.

No quincy belly, head straight
the body as balanced as mercury.
Eye to eye, face to face transmission.

The drum in everyone beats.
I am seated, only watching
my heart racing for my youth.

As We Draw Ourselves (2008)

A Long Swim

Swimming out there
Musculature in ultramarine
In weed-green sea
You can think 'mackerel'
Till you're blue in the face
But you go like tow rope—
Heavy, frayed, stretched
From pier to pier
From year to year

Entering at the southern one
Mind finned with intent
Crossing crags and sea-grass
Gutters gouged by ebb tides
Rays much wider than beds
Their glide-aways heavenly
Over sands that cloud the hourglass
In light that breaks the light
Squid invisible, abalone opalescent
The flood tide your freedom
Its reverse your test of worth

Emerging at the northern one
Your body out of water
Your flesh, on arrival
The underside of flounder
Each tooth in your head
A little colder, your sense
Of time like coral

Old Photo: The Union Buries...

A solid pack around his grave.
Good steel to a magnet, the sky leaden
with the warmth, somehow, of common ground.

I did not know them all
but the bulk of them knew me. Their leader
told them of his bookish son

and of his grand children gathered—see,
near my elbow on the lava plain
on the hard crust of the flats

near thistles, stone walls, *Carbon Black*
and the cracker's flame leaping
where the cranes once flew

over a lad's lizard-hunting days.
That was the time of solid stories,
of organizing rather than mourning.

This group, with family in it, is resolution.
I remember stupidly thinking, the clay's so
sticky no union man could turn in it.

A Mackerel Green Sea

To make such poems—
with pipes and ladders you can see
a dream of public flame leaping, jetting
licking and turning inside out
from the cracker called speech
(a refinery itself
distilling the crude
the non-degradable, the ephemeral)—
to put these things *out*
has a kind of steam-power ease to it.

In fact, to write corporately
is certainly pleasant
and has its own aesthetic—
like eating ice cream at the wheel of a fast car
or in front of a B & O TV—
which is to say
it is as manufactured
as Blake's naming of mills
his petroleum-jelly Satan
and harvest of fields
a landscape his *terms*
as much as anything
rolled out like a bowling green.

If I could say, contra Culture,
that leftisms swim well
in a mackerel green sea
I might retire now.
But they do not.
Anymore than I can just
call up Mayakovsky or hire
a revolver or imagine
angels over the Pentagon.

Necessity: Poems 1996-2006 (2007)

Still, the sea, here before me
has a sheen, scales that knit
shimmer in gill and wind-fin
with a heave of truth in it
and which seems, well... right.

Think of Walt's late dictum:
that if he could if he would trade
the greatest poets and their works
for one wave upon the shore.

He said that not meaning to
shut himself down, so didn't.
His lines rolled on
over plains, mountains, down rivers
just as the Left rolls on, after a fashion.

I can't tell as I speak
if I'm buffed in its wake
its sound-system or both
or, somehow, air-born—
emitted from the rackety tower
we built to process History
when History can become...
well ... polystyrene.

So light, these words
if you can keep them light.
Hardy, if you crack them the right way.

I Know a Poet with a Gun

A Luger.
In a cigar case.
In a cabinet
smelling of Cologne.

It's a beauty.
As Monroe and Brando were.
And Dietrich
with her holder.

The poet
does not want the gun
for culture wars
We have none to speak of.
The Americans have won.

It's horrific
the thought that I
separate the revolver
from those smoking chimneys.
But I do.

In Stalingrad
I hope that gun
was buried in snow.
Sad that it's here but true
and forcing some questions.

What does the poet want?
Love, and money.

When does he want it?
Now. For his power
has gone without saying.

Its magazine is oiled
with that sexy click
to it. Weight in
the hand a hammer has.

It's not often you
want to kill someone
but if you do here's a fine thing
to talk with, commune with
and attune.

But no, O no.
There's always the telephone
in the cold hall.
Mayakovsky where are you?

The poet knows that
in the beginning was the deed.
He must combat this.
and remain useless.

from The War Sonnets

The Waiting

When the war starts our yacht races
will be over. It will be the New Year.
Our raggedy Christmas trees
will be taken down with a rueful thought
for the months to come. We will feel older, as you
Mr President, might flourish as The Younger.

We will do our best to bear witness
to your escalating return to the crib.
That the zoo just raised their chimp
is a thing that might help us through.
Our summer is your victim's winter, as you,
with a bat's flutter, wave to vermin crew—
the cameramen who know you, and the few
who pay you. May the crater engulf you.

Suburban drought, grief, a peace plan

Drought set father against son
on behalf of the grandfather who had rain.
Declaring my childhood place a slum,
I berated, with the wrath of the old
campaigner, my son the student tenant.
A sour thunder settled in the radical clay.

Grotesque—the way agapanthus bloomed
and mother's roses barely grew.
But after our squall quiet came:
he absorbed the word 'neglect',
I took up the larger shame and
a peace plan surfaced: to toil
shoulder to shoulder with the old spades
restoring the garden, ignoring the war for oil.

Strangely Proud

In these dread-filled times I think
of my Red Uncle and his sweaty didacticism:
his hungers, his obliviousness to food while talking,
his laughter when he mentioned Chaplin,
his handshake, that grip, when it was Lenin
'Who never made a mistake, no—never.'

In New Guinea my uncle was the engineer
who blew up bridges. After the war, the designer
of a non-petrol engine every firm rejected. After Petrov,
an insomniac. One winter, his mind on fire
and certain of the Mormons in his rear vision,
he swam the Goulburn River. He was admitted,
hid his pills, confided in my father. Fenced with them,
I was strangely proud behind the wire.

Copy and Copy

After one hand-held video too much
you're driven outside to try your luck
with your own writing
even on to a shed door:

Soldiers who wish to be a hero
Are practically zero
But those who want to be civilians
Jesus, they run into millions

So said WW2 graffiti
in a US Army latrine
which so pleases you you copy it freehand
you copy and copy, writing in hope.
Then, like a Marine back from leave
memory lets go of the rope.

Rumi's Dancing Shoes

I read my poems in Perth's Persian heat
the kind of heat that puts a lid on argument
and leads to sleep or treachery or war.
I can feel my categories melting.
How stale the modern activist rhetoric.
Too easy it is to hate back.
My mouth tastes like dog meat.

My father used to say, 'like this', and
cupping a hand over his teeth, exhaled
to check on his own breath. Then,
a blacksmith pounding on History's anvil, he'd say
those heavy principled things all over again. Whereas

I want my words, like Rumi's dancing shoes
to be alight with hope.

from Flint: Gramsci in Prison

At Ustica (off Palermo, winter, 1926)

                 A slow crossing
Nature was against you going
                the ferryboat driven back by storms
                three times you had to return
                as if to say:
from one prison to another we go
                like Ariel
                like Prospero

                But the welcome of the island wind
it blows with you from one side to the other
as free as a bird a man is
                and most unlike (Kipling would say)
                those burnt alive
                      prematurely thrown into a ditch
                      left for dead

A man in a cottage.
                He wants only
                a small coffee glass
or he will make his own set
                from eggshells

Go on reading   reading
            make your library delicate and strong
                a raft of shells
only a few hours of resentment when they turned the lights off in our cells

A good man with his strong box
                wants only a safety razor
                a small file
                a bottle of aspirin
in case the strong winds give me inflammation of the gums

He reads and eats
                eats twice as much
                              is fat on words, sinewy sentence
slim on the severance from his shy wife, the children:
Dear Giulia, do, please, write…

To write one letter well is to reinvent electricity
                Sparks in the molecules

The One (Milan, winter 1926)

Who am I without you
                only one?
Only one who does not write
                I lose my name
or fame mispronounces me
Gramasci, Granusci. Gramisci. Gramasci
                even *Garamascon*—
vital but
        you would think it
                    anarcho-syndicalist speech

In the baggage room
        out of the wind on the island
a man called himself
                the Only One
I am the Only One, he told his captors
I am the Only One, was all he said to them:
                Prince of prisoners

I am your one
I am the only one
        without property
                is what he meant—
that speaker, a Sicilian
        a criminal
        tough as leather

Necessity: Poems 1996-2006 (2007)

Gramsci? he said, Antonio?
                You cannot be!
            I can be, I said
squirt though I am
the famous deputy Gramsci
      who rises each day
             cleans his toilet, drinks
              half a litre of warm milk
reads, ambles, smokes
                    reads and
I have *a fond hug* for those who can…

Dear Giulia
find the current though their own
                    case of nerves
              only one
dear one that I am
and you are…

Let me try to amuse you with another story.
I have a new guard, a kind NCO—
                know what he reads?
            Equilibria degli Egoismi

Sparrows (Milan, summer 1927)

He's a poor village
      kid again
      a hungry high school boy
      a scholar about to faint
            shivering with ideas
yet still setting himself tasks

I make movements that exercise all the joints and muscles
                systematically
and increase the number of movements gradually each week

His examination of the self as
        a sparrow alights
                the first the most
                        likeable
                for serious study

which would allow me to see all possible relationships
        in the material at hand
        and to set them
                in a harmonious order

It perches on the cork of the tamarind bottle
        a little lord
                no one can touch
he would rebel fiercely
he would peck and dance off
        princely
                sparrow and man
                eye to eye
                in their sit-in
until one day
        paralysed on his right side
he had to drag himself painfully to eat and drink then suddenly he died.
        Now a new one sits on a man's toes
        nestles in the cuff of his trousers
eats soggy bread like a man
        who cannot spell the word leather
                who prison has defeated—
it will die too
        after being
        quite nauseating in his domesticity

Dear Mother
do you remember our childhood dare when we hammered our fingers
with stones until a drop of blood came out at the finger tips?

Necessity: Poems 1996-2006 (2007)

from Getting the Revolution Straight

Overture

When the killings had to start
—taking the Winter Palace, storming the Bastille—
they seemed like postscripts
to a story long in the writing.

Say the catechism after me.
Rousseau. Marx. Lenin ... No.
Socrates. Erasmus. Diderot...
Start again. Tom Paine.

The Rosaries of analysis. Reasonings.
Can we be as plain as the alphabet?
Abstractions are the Bastille.
(Ah, but which ones?)

A matter of claiming the rights of words.
In soliloquising, hold on to
the semicolon. There are nightingales
in expectant clauses, and line

breaks that sketch the ghostly
body of the poem. Invisible cities.
Aurora over the lights in them.
Pink lagoons, martinis. The clarity

that's in ideals when
you give them the shake
that is the poem. Come then,
down the Arno with Shelley,

from Alpine hope descending
as far as Pisa,

and Pound's end
(collapse of the *Analects*).

The *Don Juan* sinking under full
sail. Divorce! Divorce! a sign
of knowledge in our times,
says the good Doctor WCW.

Our doctor, under the wattle,
shed no blood for the ballad,
another good thing—like seeking
the melody of thinking,

a key to concepts. *Communitas*.
Naming the start of the story,
the better to gauge its possible
ending, which seems to be now.

A moment. Like Kronstadt.
Kronstadt came from—?
where does ice come from if not water
which is all around us?

Kronstadt: the revolution's pure chance
of reform from within. But what,
citizen, does the inside of an idea
look like? Pinning *that* down might be

a windfall into the next century.
Body surfing from Rousseau on.
But it would *feel* like turning
your guts inside out.

Say Lenin with a contemplative face,
and people think you're the Elephant Man.
Say Stalin, and you're dead.
The numbers won't go in the head.

Necessity: Poems 1996-2006 (2007)

Swapping death masks,
is that the way to go?
Maybe yes, maybe no.
I don't *know*.

This is not farce we're in.
It's still History

Poland

This land, like a depression,
will steal your youth and turn it into a password.
                                    —Adam Zagajewski

Plato's dictum:
knowledge as remembrance.
Have I been here before?
I walk into the shape
of an idea, ease the tired foot
into its straps, only to slip
on the cobbles
end up in the ditch.
Start again. Think more.

Standing beside headstones
in bright summer,
my shadow is as solid
though they are scattered,
broken or bent with cruel neglect.
Maybe that's it
a matter of motionlessness.
When I agitate equations,
when things multiply
by three or six,
or even seven million,
I fall into History.

I know this now.
I wrote it down
after hearing it
everywhere except here.
I said particulars to myself
they become general and
here I am among these fields
with an old dirt road

running between them.
And what I have said
blows like a breeze
as if it is new and mine;
though its ground is known
and never new.

Do come in
sit down to the Old News.
Make yourself
at home in dialogue
where re-cognitions bloom.
In speech we harvest poppies
as whole fields of knowledge.
Light up, that's the spirit,
there's time to burn.
Concentrate, and remember.
You know it all already.

And here comes a dray.
I have seen that before,
or something very like it.
It's drawn by Hercules in amber:
he snorts along the dusty road.
The owner sways to and fro, and
walking behind, I can smell
the man and his valiant horse,
the horse of a man,
and the horse's manly sweat,
their heads and necks strained
and leathered as a harness;
and the whip that flicks
along the spine of the horse,
as distinct from the man's.

Must the crack of that whip
—its stinging sound

its single stroke
its dash, its unit
into the flesh—
be less a single event in my mind
than an echo of some kind?

Ah, "of some kind".
The sound dies away,
doesn't it. What's left?
A species of what I have
not named, of what I fear
is here in the sunshine.
What I heard was what I said it was,
and is as much more than itself
as the sky, just as the blue
of the sky is greater than the sky,
as blue itself encompasses the sky's
blue in favour of the whole idea,

an abstract measure which
might conceivably encompass
the whip I mentioned.
I write this for the present
 as if for the first time,
holding to my dray of statement,
 my load of the illusory present,
that groans in History, in bridled guilt.

Further along the road,
the scene repeats itself.
How many Hercules
can a man carry
in his mind at once?
The lovely heavy lidded
eyes of this horse shine:
"they were the days".
There are motionless peasants

everywhere. Potatoed.
Is that a bag of spuds
asleep under a tree?
Now I've seen everything.

Absolute and Real
in summer Poland
in the dark light
of the country road
delivering cart after cart
and the inevitable next cart
commanded by the whip
back through the dust
of all the summers
to lash after lash
in the gorgeous light,
where the ripe rye hums
and there is a haze over
every golden middle distance.

Knowledge returns me
to the harness of History
where everything
has already happened.

That's how it is
when I think I think
I know, even when
I'm looking up and around
to see what *is* or *was*
the other side of this field,
at the end of the road,
back there, beyond these
languid instances: yes,
for a moment,
only a glimpse,
mind you.

The glare of summer dazzles
even after aeons at
the fire of remembrance.

It's enough to make you
drag yourself and all
that you have or had
back inside the cave;
as a dray goes past,
one I recognise (again!)
from the pattern of splintered
spokes, not the grain
of wood in the driver's seat,
some details are invisible
in the general, the light
out there is tricky…
And the terrifying thought
comes to mind:
of something unique,
something absolutely
defying categories.

Look at the poppy.
The one by the empty vodka bottle.
Flower that pollinates forgetfulness.
The single one, with its shy stem,
its red swaying above it
like nothing else
now or ever.

Then the moment passes.
Gone like a gulp.
And so there is
red everywhere, the red of reds,
there is a field of blood out there,
that is the truth. In bright summer
we forge away and know

Necessity: Poems 1996-2006 (2007)

it's there without looking.
How? Hail Pure Reason and
the hammering of qualities.
The hammering of qualities
makes the world. What mould
for what metal shall we pour
all the howling into? Manifold
metals, cities of moulds.

I've got my head down now,
toiling at lines that won't
flare with too much History.
It's a noisy place to be
(even in the countryside),
but that's how it is. I'm
in the roar of certainty.
Same with everybody here.

The furnace is my life, the fire
we're in is *a priori*. We look around,
and we have, with familiar skills,
shaped some words ready to be shod.
White hot, they hang on hooks.
I can hear the horses approaching.
One neighs, I can't tell which.
Someone relishes the whip.
I couldn't name the man.
I hear the crack and
think I feel a cut close
to the creature's bone,
its burn of recognition.

And we're near the Bug
—a particular that takes nothing
away from remembrance:
some rivers love the heat
of memory. Blood fermented,

they gently wend
between numbers.

But that poppy
the one near the bottle,
even the *idea* of it is
harder than glass to swallow.

Honey Ant

Eating honey ant
is tasting bitterness at first.
You put its tail on your tongue
acrid tip to acrid tip, then
you put the living thing further in.
A golden bubble, like a promise
swells behind the teeth
and fills your mouth
with common sweetness.
But there's nothing to compare
with the bursting
that is to each taste
and is as it dissolves
a tear of nectar.

Noon

Blues in their eyes burn
in ether of patience, strange sacrifice.

Each endure their trance
of solid starlight, their Milky Way.

No rock in shadow
All days exposed.

In this ancient inland sea
obligation is shedding its skin.

And still she is swollen
with honey—wild bounty.

Ribs

There are wave formations
    in the archaic rocks.
        Fish ripple
            in shoals of salt.

In the throbbing heat
    a gauze of light
        dresses wounds
            names the hours.

Satellite photographs
    show blue blood—
        thinking veins all over:
            bodies of song
                in ribs of ranges.

This place is made
    for matrimony
        it's laid out
            with trust in time.

Chant
    and snakes
        are rainbows.

The Inland Sea (2001)

Songs and Escarpments

Their sweet dark juice is flowing forth;
From the centre of the chalice it's flowing forth

From the slender pistil it is flowing forth;
The sweet dark juice is flowing forth

Let our sap encircle them with rings;
Let the flood of nectar encircle them

Let our sweet sap ooze from the ground...

*

High blown—Strehlow's diction in *Songs of Central Australia*.

As a lover of antiquity, a seeker of eternity, he was in tune with the Hebrew habit of couplets, where lines lie parallel with each other, one arm around the other, in skilful repetition.

The golden braid that couplets make as they dance down a page.

His translations rooted him in this place, as a love of love watered the *Song of Songs*.

The translator as celebrant.

*

One day we walked in crystals, out onto the salt lake.
Come on, I said, this way.
We were still in love, I think.

Footsteps, like words found in translation, led us towards the
    centre.
Except, as in translation, no centre was possible; it could not be
    reached, word by word.
Behind us was some notion of the original.
Out there, towards the middle, the crust gave way.
Very slowly we had to turn back.
But we pressed on around the salt lake, stepping lightly on the
    succulents.

*

See—
Beside a wall he stands
Shows himself
Glancing through the lattice

*

The bell bird relentlessly rouses her
The dark-chested one relentlessly rouses her

The bell bird fills her with madness
The dark chested one fills her with madness…

Her desires she encloses with a fence—
A thicket shuts her in like a fence.

Underground Rivers Running

If only you would speak to me
If only you would say something in this heat
If only you would pick up that stone and sing
    pluck the bones out of your throat
    hear my pauses between lines
If only you would laugh at the right time
    digest my body well
    go and stay with me always
If only you would leave me alone in you
If only you would see me for what I am by the river
    hunt my gaze down each time
    let my breath cool yours
    your breath raise my body
If only the animals that pass between us spoke
If only the bird on my shoulder was uncaged
If only each of our words had the same root
If only our children would dance with each other
If only we had the same day to make the journey
If only you knew exactly what I new
    and what you know I believed absolutely, effortlessly.
If only you could make my time flow to music
If only you had no greater need for sweetness that me
If only we could pass in and out of each other like water
    and all weathers united us
    and drought was a blessing
    and my fire did not consume you
               or yours mine
If only your river filled my river with nectar
If only we could be the flood, and flood each other
    with no risk of drowning
If only underground rivers ran through us

Riverbed Song

Late one night, as I was walking over the Todd River where there are, these days, many deaths. I looked down from the bridge and saw something wonderful. It was young couple, still unscarred by rough living.

In moonlight I saw them.
Two in a swag
under the bridge.
His royal sleep.
Her hair flowing
over his happy arm.
A good cattle dog
guarding their marriage.

Much later, when I saw a cover illustration of the *Song of Songs* the connection was made. It showed a couple lying face to face, their eyes closed, their arms about each other, like parallel couplets. Naked above the waist, and united below by bed clothes.
The original image was in alabaster, the lid of an Etruscan sarcophagus. In the line of the carving you could see the *Song of Songs* flowing back into the death cult.

Back

Returning inland, seasons later
                a lizard waits for me.
Clatter in the kitchen.
                    Length across the frying pan.

I thought its thump and scuttle
                a bird on the roof.
It has striped rings, runnels of sand down its tail.
                Eyes like ants.

I tried to ignore it, and it's off
                in timely spurts.
Wish I had suction pads
                and tongue-in-groove
moves along the ceiling

around the room, behind paintings
                Black Cockatoo Dreaming
then under the big *Ewaninga*
                increase place—

lizard with honeyed toes.
            Cheeky fat one
that one, plump as corkwood…

it's belly on the nail
              hanging the *Men's Business*
Waterhole high under the bark
            painting in the corner

where I'm trying to sleep
            in a crappy chair.

Road Train

To have warm wide breasts
        like that woman
                crossing the highway
letting the young men go ahead
        gangly with fire wood
                knowing as they do
exactly how many breaths
        of daylight are left
                in this glorious, glowing
suspense of things
        before night—
                The way the country
used to tell you
        everything
                if you waited right.

She steps out
        arms akimbo
                four dingo pups in a row
jigging along at her bosom
        the fold of each
                flapping ear
dusty fur at her throat
        perambulating
                all scent and muzzle
and their being no
        spirit there
                to call out, to warn her
of the giant snarl
        the roaring
                Road Train.

Good Ship Calcutta

Prosperous winds of Santa Cruz:
Devil may-care
loincloths and silks
say i am innocente

All the scents of Rio:
lime juice, plums, vinegar,
almond dry decks
say i am innocente

Capt'n Collins boxed at the opera
with poxy Hannah Power
and Fanny Anchor
say i am innocent

A pound of fresh meat
six oranges a day
and no Frenchman's Disease
say i am innocent

Print of tiger's paw
dens of wolves
at Simon's Town
say i am innocente

Death in Roaring Forties
three heifers buckling
their moaning udders
say i am innocente

Turkeys, ducks, capons
geese, pigs, Cape sheep
with stringy wool
say i am innocent

Ghosting William Buckley (1993)

All winter down wind:
squawk and bellow
on Noah's Ark
say i am innocente…

Beyond that
one thing i did steal:
a bolt of Irish cloth
though no dolt am i

if a lump of clay
they'd say…
i was a lump of clay
to mark their words

Escaping

1.

With each step we make
                history on unthinking feet
                      through mind scrub—
we progress, crossing as best we can
                projections of streams
                      and full rivers of mourning:
from that antipodean depression
                at Sullivan's Bay, saddles
                      of dune, dead water in casks
mosquitoes breeding to a pitch
                men bloodied one way or
                      another—under leaden skies
on Christmas Day, we raised a hatch
                and lurched out:
                      James Taylor, William Vosper
Daniel McAlenan, William Marmon and me,
                one scuttling Celt and Englishmen.

                Native fires in the distance.
Smoke spiralling as we stumbled towards
                rank creeks, tangles
                      of our fearful and free parting.
Avoiding the bay, its scum of shore, its rashy
                noggins of sandstone
                      ash bone, shell pits, carting a gun
and iron kettle we veered
                inland in prickly incomprehension
                      of detour—
rations gone in two days
                of creek bashing and circling
                      no peaks visible four days out:

a few fresh water tricklings
        a fair enough river between trees, eye-opening
            onto a plain, a crust
of possibilities due west:
        two molars in the hard jaw—
            vantage points
to the mind's eye…
        Skeletal, spent, we climbed
            scabby moss on lizard granite
blue-tongues hanging out
        as we reached the top
        boulders
only to see—
        more damned plains!
            Stubble and whatnot
except for, back the way we'd come—
        a coinage of sea, an inlet glinting
            then dulling to pewter
something to come down to
    at dusk and the
        cannibalistic opossum cries.
And in the morning—
        claypan, quicksand
            our progress hostage to Mother
Nature
        McAlenan's swamp sounds
            as we came, finally
to sand-grit, ti-tree and the fact of return
        as if memory as good as beached us
            in the same cursed place!
For there
        over the bay on its shore
            was our ship and settlement.

Vosper wept.
        Marmon bellowed beside Taylor's curdling joy.
            Why I fancied

I could see Capt'n Collins on parade
        raising the flag half-mast
                in honour of our absence, perhaps
since we had come full circle, almost.
        We set about making signals
                lighting a fire that night
by day hoisting shirts on trees
        until a boat was seen
                to embark in our direction.
Dread of punishment is great
        yet fear of starvation
                exceeds it
when you crave deliverance.
        Half way across
                towards our swelling hopes
of relief and perhaps forgiveness
        by the Governor—
                the longboat slowed, went about
and was heading back before
        a man could say *lash*.
                The patched sail unfurled and
the westerly blew that rescue
        back to place of our captivity.
                And to this day
        I cannot explain this.
                Nor could the others
who were thumping the sand
        like seals expiring.

2.

When companions leave you walk around
yourself for a bit, you thank Providence
for buttonholes and a firm lining
of crutch to see you through.
There is scratchiness of vigour, too.

As they waded off, deserting this squelch
of island, I noticed two oyster catches
winging their way home over the sea grass.
There are, I thought, creatures stationed here
with fat regard for revelation.

I took pause about my guilty
big feet in the old country, how
trembling yet grateful I was to join
the regiment. Then I jollied again the low flame.
In stripping down we have ourselves to blame.

In the evening, that night, I wept.
I kept dreaming that when I woke
the old tide of vanity would be right out
that the light next morning would be Deliverance
for one in thanksgiving for dry reeds, warm sands.

In point of fact, I breakfasted on bones
of the dead, which is to say thoughts
of my newly departed convict mates, the
rats and scabs and cowards—
wondering if, at the height

of my hopelessness, I would break the glass
of the question this bay asks. Then I thought
of my mother, a thing I seldom do.
Once spurned, we are sandpipers
on mud as far as our thin legs will carry us…

That morning I counted
ninety–six cormorants on mangrove stumps
and saw not one wallaby
between myself and the sea—
another mark of Providence.

Ghosting William Buckley (1993)

At a Pinch

They were a clump of trees.

Then against one trunk
        an arm beside a greasy thigh
        moved a finger. Tweaked.
Who are you?
            The man to step forward
            was the tallest and strongest
            but a feather on the rough grass.
            And he was down-wind
            no sound to him and no scent either
            as they closed upon each other
Buckley still, Buckley's gaze
            as alert as the welts
            on the other's cheeks, shoulders, chest.

Each of the waiting clan held still.

Two greeting fingers fixed on Buckley's belly
and the *pinch*, that was the word
        was a bosun's whistle, half-heard.

In return, a trembling Buckley was allowed
        to touch a filthy thatch.

O the unscarred, terrified features of Buckley there
        when the black hand flattened on his chest
        pink flesh on pink flesh
        where armour might have been, but wasn't
nothing shielded his abdomen
        the warrior squeezing
        and pulling him like rope
        testing him amidships.

Buckley judged he had to root
each foot deeper into ground
as he was eased about and around —
held, patted, stroked
           incising
           thumb nail in the split
                of calf muscle
                     in the run of thigh to hip bone—
a slice of appreciation here
a round of anticipation there?

           Buckley hoped not, he sought
           dumb solace from the distant
           horizon, he was stock still
           for the first man, forbearing for the next
           the other one's brother in thoroughness
           each making putty
           of his flesh
           not knowing, as yet,
           the quality of Buckley's kidney fat.

Buckley fixed as clay during this possession
           not yet to knowing, either
           his arrival confirmed, yes
                          as spirit.

They showed him the spear of a dead brother he carried.
They pinched, again and again, his white skin returned from
the dead.

Magpie

Listen to your *Barroworn* now.
He is singing you up in morning light.
He is wrapping you round in magic.
He lifted you from caves of being white
Transforming your inheritance.

See him hop from bough to bough.
That in his beak is not a snake.
It's a tool, a charm to dig up hope.
A breeze blows to his fancy
He carols, he sports with return.

Sing with the bird your freedom.
Celebrate your shipwreck.
Sing with a spirit of tattered pride
to the young black woman you lie beside:
she's full fathom, and your aerial eye.

Eel

She speaks to me of *Bornea*
I flick and slide under weeds
until she nets me up, and lets me dry
on the bank of Despond, then
the skin of my failings silken
and a slippery line of trust
firms between us.
Bornea is slit-eyed, willing, lithe
sweet white meat cooked on coals.

Promiscuous

Anguila Australis Surgeon once said.
Born in tropical seas, *Leptophallus* drawn
to cooler waters. *Lepto*—thin, slender
they flow south to new waters
pushing upstream into narrower
ways, in their intestinal quest
                    to swell and grow there.
                    Yellowing.
                    Gold in nets.
                    Bornea
which fatten after rain
and in vigour return, strive back
in creeks, rivers, through lakes again
                    to the sea.
                    Silvered
Bornea in ocean moonlight…
                    A man might think
gold into silver won't go
anymore than, say,
white into black or spirit
into a living body
                    of a woman.
                    To think that
the mixing in this upside-down land
is erroneous, if not
                    felonious. Why
                    a fish can have
hind parts of a shark with
a skate's head. A bird has
straight legs, the feet of a parrot
a beaver-like-thing
                    the feet of a duck:
such is the great Southern

promiscuous intercourse of
creatures, vegetables, flowers.

    So what chain
of Being is it
       with you in it?

I am lithe with intermingling thoughts—
    see black hulks again
       feathered and floating on this
swan bay, such ship-of-state birds but
          black not white
their tubular necks musically transported
    in the prow of
          Kunnawarra Kunnawarra

their cooing ease across the sea grass—
orgy of grazing and scarlet
      slash of wing
        tucked under song…

muddying my waters
stirring me up to I don't know what.
    Invisible seethings of song—
the tide running quickly strange, fast and present.

Tattoo

I hurl a stone at the bird
        hating its cruel
beak. I am alone. They have
        for some strange reason
taken their ceremonies from me.
        I scrounge at camp.

One of the dogs.

        Idly, I smear
with forefinger and thumb—
painting myself.
A doodling aftermath
        of myself. Pipeclay.

        Painted—
a face stares at death
it lives with death
dies in its own eyes
        if eyes can see.

        A bitch arrives
to skinny-sniff
        the mourning mask—
hard to know what to most
        lament : convict settlement
or a childhood so distant
        memory is primitive.

        Squinting, you
take hold of your own
        hand, wrist, forearm:
you imagine
        a W and a B

Ghosting William Buckley (1993)

and fancy a man
        needs a moon
to see him through
        a sun
a bird that's not
        his confounded totem.
And, what the hell
        why not give yourself
a whimpering furry companion.

        Cut and press.
        Hold and slice.
See how we make our own mark.
Clay can seal a wound.
        The sun blazes
        with blood besides
        my slice of moon.

Koim

I was driven out of my native country
by a dreadful sound in mine ears.
        —John Bunyan, *The Pilgrim's Progress*

Koim is thumping the grass with their tails
Koim is thumping grass and standing still
They are sitting up and scratching bellies with paws
They scratch and thump the grass with their tails
Their tails thick and warm to touch, lying on the grass
Fat on the grass like snakes, *Koim* thumping
The grass seeds, flattening them in the sun
The warm tails of *Koim* thumping the grass down
The bellies of *Koim* thick-furred and scratched
They scratch with their claws and their tails thump seed…

On Civilization's Platter

Stepping into their camp, in undulating amnesia, deaf to
your mother tongue, standing like a child waiting for Master
to speak. Gaze oceaned, the tide of your old chatter
right out, faithfulness sucked back
making of you a clump in the ti-trees
a lump of clay for a wheel they turn
to recognize their ghost, their navvy of misfortune
some hewer of banishments
their spectre of Caliban, waiting for himself to say.

You and your new scent on the breeze. The tongue
like a rope slung from one root
to another root until a word *did* come—
flicked out of incredulity, and dangled over
the threat of mistaken identity, or no identity
whatsoever: (no name for these plains of scrub
        no name for the iron beaked whiteblack bird
        no name for deadness of lava
        the lead of time in it...)

The word that rafted the equator and humidly established itself
in a tropic of gainful recognition. A single utterance
to lightly plumb, like a crumb sinking in water
its own sound, floating downwards
into the star circuits of fish brain, bone
marrow cord of electric connection—
the right intermingling at last

Coming into their camp you heard the word *Bread*.

Bread. And your memory, like a whale off-shore, stirs.
Bread. The spout breaks the blue surface.
Bread. You gullet opens to harvest the krill

Ghosting William Buckley (1993)

that animates the seas as the land is sung
by your Wothaurung friends...
                              Bread.

Ovens roar in a man's breast, though privately
—kindling words, green trees you called by name—
memory's in bloom, though buried somewhat
by fear of the spoken, dread of your own voice
back from the dead, garden beds of Virtue
to be cultivated all over again, Providence permitting.

Bread. Drawn slowly out of your own archaic tongue.
Bread. Its old warmth on civilization's platter.

Dune

Dear one, I want to put my head where yours is
in the moonlight, night wind warming the grass
silver pouring over your cheeks, lengthening your lashes.

When I re-order myself to be still, absolutely
quiet in opposition to your abandonment
—your arms out, hip lost to a dent—
there's a hollow beneath me, an emptiness
as if I have, while propped up to see the horizon
fallen back into the dune where you nested yourself.

A while ago, in the dark, I experimented with patience.
I lay with my face touching the invitation
of your hand, trying myself out finger-printed, almost
for life, a mark of the exchanges we practise
as we sleep and (let's face it) when we wake:

no silver then, the moon swings about to look skinned
above the rising sun. The ocean's slaps, its new tide
makes no comment on the naturalness with which we pretend
to forget each other, a forgetfulness that renders
every lover as the same lover no matter what
so swart the sea is when we are in it.

Raft (1990)

Downpour

In the kiss, as it rains
they eat of rosemary
and scent of lemon thyme.

In the kiss, as he cups
her skull, she knows trees
are besotted by autumn
will give all to winter.

Her hand on him
moves to return the breath
he gives and give again
in the downpour
of their silence.

In the glinting foliage
in the wet bark and in the sap
there is silence risen
from rustlings, twitterings:
two trees, a choir of forest.

And there is no change.
It is a sonata of light rain.
It will never cease
this mouth by mouth necessity.

As if, in the wakening
by the open garden gate
each is turning and turning
the other's face around
in search of the ones they had
before they were born.

Raft (1990)

Banquet

You are such a beauty.
Layers keep coming off us.
Skins. Luscious peelings of surprise.
So that even when we part
hours later, and my hands
for those dumb reasons of a day
must be wiped of you,
and when your face ripening
over/under mine no longer
glows in my inward gaze
I am like some native yam
like your regular home-grown tuber
that sugar/starch tropical root
food still swollen for you:
and swelling as I say this,
mouthful after mouthful.

Hope

1
This afternoon, a fog came in from the sea
as swiftly as a smile fades. Radiance in the bowl
of sand where the kids played; then cold grey.

2
The foghorn started up. Out of the wooden hut
near the lighthouse, sound rips and tears, smashing
hope. They thought it land's end.

3
We bundled into the car together. Is that
the moon up ahead, or the sun blazing on
our promised land? Don't look at it for long.

4
The fog lingered. In patches it promised and
procrastinated. That giant mound of salt
our favourite landmark, turned Antarctic pink.

From My Daughter's Blood

Inside the veins there are navies setting forth,
Tiny explosions at the water lines,
And seagulls weaving in the wind of the salty blood.
                                        Robert Bly

1 This Morning

In the blue morning air you turn your
fingertips up, asking me not to select
the little one. I try the thumb, like some
calloused thumb of my heart, aorta of blame
and succeed, almost, in pricking me instead
of you. But you, you are still there
in your gown, eskimo slippers and trust
in the fat drop that will come—swollen, expectant
its Jacobean globule balanced as mercury
on the skin we keep aslant the light:
your index finger I have now to squeeze,
the Buddha candle flickering
as we sit, minds incensed, jetting
tapering into one breath, the radio on.

2 Actrapid (Insulin)

This *thing's* steely finesse hurls
travellers into a sea-ice Space Future
where there's no eye, either
just a sliver of entry.
Cylinders fill on Planet Efficiency, well.
Calibrations of Pig Juice suck up the day, well.
Time-trek ends with incisive penetration
of all mind, flesh, star-dust
—imagine: prospects upheld to a single point
a prick with which to inject all god's creatures as one…
There, love. Done!

Hippocrates

Look, here is my thigh for you to jab
if you want. Nothing to it. In their own way
Dads have to be thick-skinned for this.
And now it is done again, see.
It's off, the squeal in it smothered
as it courses through you, its invisible
spill and spread as positive as skin lotion
will be when you are thirteen
and doing *it all for yourself:*
from sugar tests to disposal jobs
—the walking off from him as he, if he
cares for you, will stay to put leavetakings away…

Hippocratically, I collect the fluffy
Bloodied little wads, bin them. Then we've gone
leaving no trace of transpositions.

Idea of Absence

Gone from the garden now.

There is where she wandered
in clumps of sodden grass
to be mown after storms
a hiatus between plastic
chairs under the lime canopy
of the walnut tree—
by cups, balls, dolls
that she gathered busily
squatting and running naked
her hair tied at the nape
(that bare slice of her mother).

Heading for the red swing.

How long will she keep
her first, short sharp teeth
and trust to call me?

I step out in her absence
try to wander ahead of myself.
The air's crisp, the seed
boxes are battered
on the breathing soil.
I lie down in the trembling
aftermath of rain, gather
myself in again and see
as I recline
not dilapidations but her
seeking to hide the idea
of absence from me:

Raft (1990)

as in first light on waking
I thought it a kitten's paw
tentatively on my cheek
and found her popped up
her head out of covers
her face beside mine, for me:
'Look, I am not
to be lopped off, see…'

Horticulture

I asked the X
why it is
the walnuts
break open
to an ashy pulp.
Because, she said
you haven't split
the tree's bark.

Dim Sim Time

1
You don't want to say it, even to yourself.
It's too hard and may not even be true but it
has to be said: she didn't love you enough.
Same with the other woman. Not enough love
to meet what you wanted to give and probably
did give. O the miserable waters that flow
in Taoist lore. What comes now? A river
a lake, an ocean of grief? The Chinese had
water clocks. They had a natural flow—
the drops into ladles of seasons
rolling round to mill harmonizing truths.
Think. Before Hamilton's mainspring, before
Cook's longitudinal transit of Venus
no one time served life's design.

2
You might think I'm a sucker for geography—
over-circumscribed by domestic compass
a kind of Magellan without his Pacific
Panamas of pathos blocking progress...

Well, there's some truth in that. I eat cheese
burgers too, as well as brown rice and lychees.
'Cloudy but fine' is on the label of this bottle of
brewed ale. Cheers. And I'll tell you another thing:
that dad we saw slumped at Macca's
he was waiting for the white Toyota station-wagon
driven by she who must be obeyed borrowed
for the delivery of his smiling, waving children—
like that bloke we saw at the Go-Go counter lunch
jerking the stripper into his lap, an Access man as well.

Raft (1990)

Rope

6 a.m. and I am meditating.
The heavy rattle of the ute
as Rob and Bobbie start out.

I'm on the mat
and they are going
to the day's work of fishing.

Father and son in the same
boat. My candle burns
slowly as if to consume
the fog on the water.

Two men, chugging along
the cut, out to the sea.
Will I ever progress
at this stilling?

Who is at the tiller
I wonder. Son
Bob says, take her
towards the second light.

Sometimes I think I detect
through the mist
the other shore
ever present.

One incense stick
and they are well launched
their warm voices at rest
like rope on a deck.

Raft (1990)

Notes

'Badly Mothered, Burning Chaos'
Sam Hamill founded Copper Canyon Press and his *The Essential Chuang Tzu* was published by Shambhala.

'Murmured Conversations'-
Murmured Conversations; A Treatise on Poetry and Buddhism by the Poet-Monk Shinkei, Translation, Commentary and Annotation by Esperanza Ramirez-Christensen, Stanford University Press 2008.

New Alice Springs Poems
Hidden Valley is a slum camp north of the range in Alice Springs, where the Hayes Family live, the Native Title holders of the town. Yeperenya (Caterpillar) is the supermarket in Alice: 'life is a joyous thing with maggots at the centre' cites the anthropologist W.E.H. Stanner who wrote of the Dreaming as 'the poetic key to reality'. In the Aranda emu dance a man dangles a wooden tjurunga around his neck, signifying his heart.

Lines for Birds
John Wolseley, from 'Nettlecomb' in Somerset, arrived in Australia in 1976. He now lives in Melbourne and in the 'Whipstick Forest' near Bendigo, Victoria. His retrospective was held at the National Gallery of Victoria in 2015.

'Old Photo: The Union Buries...'
'The Union Buries Its Dead' is a classic Australian short story by the socialist writer Henry Lawson.

Ghosting William Buckley
William Buckley, born in Macclesfield, England in 1782, was tried for theft in 1802. His death sentence was reprieved to transportation for life. He escaped from his penal colony on the eastern side of Port Phillip Bay in 1803, and roamed for three decades with the Wathaurung people. Buckley rejoined 'civilization' by choice in July 1835, when he walked into the camp of the first invading pastoralists. He was an imposing 6'6" in height, of erect military bearing, with a mermaid tattooed on the up-

per part of his right arm, and on his lower right arm a sun and half moon, seven stars, a monkey and WB. He felt he had lost his language until he heard someone say 'bread.' For some years, he reluctantly acted as a go-between on the bloody frontier. He died, pardoned, in Hobart in 1856.

ACKNOWLEDGMENTS

These poems have variously appeared in journals and newspapers in the UK, USA and Australia: thanks go to the editors of *Agenda, London Review of International Law, Kenyon Review, The Literary Review, Antipodes, RePublica, Island, Cordite, Heat, Meanjin, Salt, The Age, The Australian, Arena Magazine, Overland, Dura, Art in Australia,* Black Inc's *Best Poems* as well as the publishers of poetry collections. Some poems have been revised for this book. Nourishment along the way has come, invaluably, from Graeme Bird, John Emoling, Kieran Finnane, Beverley Farmer, Rai Gaita, Joe Hill, Philip Huggins, Paul Kane, Mike Ladd, Richard Murphet, Rod Moss, Kynan Sutherland, Fay Zwicky and, as ever, my wife Rose Bygrave.

www.ingramcontent.com/pod-product-compliance
Lightning Source LLC
Chambersburg PA
CBHW022009160426
43197CB00007B/352